The Uneasy Relationship

The Uneasy Relationship

Britain and South Africa

James Barber
with an appendix by
Christopher R. Hill

Published by Heinemann for the Royal Institute of
International Affairs

Heinemann Educational Books Ltd
22 Bedford Square, London WC1B 3HH
LONDON EDINBURGH MELBOURNE AUCKLAND
HONG KONG SINGAPORE KUALA LUMPUR NEW DELHI
IBADAN NAIROBI JOHANNESBURG
EXETER(NH) KINGSTON PORT OF SPAIN

ISBN 0 435 83042 2

© Royal Institute of International Affairs 1983
First published 1983

Phototypesetting by Georgia Origination, Liverpool
Printed in Great Britain by Biddles Ltd, Guildford, Surrey

Contents

Acknowledgements

This book is one of the products of the Chatham House study group 'Southern Africa in Conflict', which met between 1978 and 1980 and was funded by the Le Poer Power Trust. Although the origins of the book are in the study group, it is not an attempt to summarize its discussions and papers. Instead it examines some of the many subjects that were discussed by the group, while James Mayall's companion volume – on South Africa in the context of the international system – will examine others.

Although the bulk of this book is concerned with Britain's relations with South Africa, Christopher Hill, another member of the group, has contributed a final section on West Germany's and France's relations with the Republic, underlining their increased importance in South African affairs. In preparing our sections, both Christopher Hill and I greatly benefited from the lively, stimulating and congenial discussions that characterized the group's meetings, but the views expressed here are our own.

I should like to acknowledge my thanks to those who gave me interviews while I was preparing the book, and my particular thanks go to Michael Spicer, who was the research officer for the group; Mrs Betty Moser, who undertook research; Miss Pauline Wickham, who has edited the book; and Mrs Cynthia Connolly and Mrs Dorothy Anson, who did much of the typing.

J.B.

1 Introduction

Of the eight statues which stand in Parliament Square in London, six are of eminent British statesmen – Canning, Churchill, Derby, Disraeli, Palmerston and Peel. One of the foreigners who stands alongside them is an American, Abraham Lincoln. The other is Jan Christian Smuts. Smuts is there for his personal achievements as soldier and statesman, but also as a reminder of the strong and continuing links between Britain and South Africa. For some Britons that is a matter of pride, but for others it is now an embarrassment. They remember Smuts not as the great international statesman, but as a racist who perpetuated a system of government based on discrimination, and South Africa not as the faithful Commonwealth member who stood by the mother country in the two world wars, but as a pariah state of the international community.

But is the relationship anything more than a residue of the past, of a now defunct imperial role? Why should South Africa be given such prominence in Britain? In Britain's changed circumstances – with membership of the European Community (EC), with a defence commitment largely confined to NATO, with no formal imperial responsibilities left in Africa and with South African trade accounting for only 2 per cent of total British overseas trade – is there any justification for the amount of attention that is given to South Africa and the passions that are aroused? This study seeks to show that there is.

Although Anglo/South African relations have been close, they have always been tense, and the tension has been within as well as between the two countries. The division among white South Africans between the Afrikaner nationalists, who resented the British links, and those Afrikaners and English-speaking whites who wanted reconciliation by working within the Commonwealth and Empire, was one of the bitterest of South African politics. Internal disputes over the relationship have been equally clear in Britain: the increased consciousness of race relations in international affairs has focused much attention on South Africa, while racial issues have become prominent in what is now a multiracial society. So far the South African question has hardly intruded into Britain's domestic race relations, but there is always the possibility that it will, and political leaders are well aware of that.

In the past the black South Africans held out hopes that the British would be able and willing to ameliorate their lot. During the shaping of the Union of South Africa, black political leaders petitioned the British monarch, complaining against the racial implications of the constitution and the laws which were enacted under it. During the two world wars, the black political parties appealed to Britain to reward the war effort of the blacks by helping their cause, but nothing came of these appeals. After the Second World War, black expectations of international support shifted to the United Nations, the Organization of African Unity (OAU) and the individual black states. However, something of the old hopes of support from Britain persisted. They were partly met – not by the government, but by the anti-apartheid and church groups, by some sections of the Labour and Liberal parties, and by the way in which London became a centre for the exiled black nationalist parties as they continued their struggle from abroad.

The presence of these vigorous groups and exiled parties has helped to keep South Africa in the forefront of British politics, and that has been reinforced by the attention given to the Republic by the British media. All this activity has increased mutual awareness, which in turn has aroused expectations. On the South African side, there is the expectation that the British should understand the country's problems better than other foreigners. Yet South African expectations conflict, for they range across race and party. If there is anger among the blacks because the British will not support the liberation movement, there is equal anger among the whites that Britain imposes an arms ban. On the British side, the moral issues that are raised bring out strong, almost crusading reactions among politicians, academics, pressure groups and newspaper editors, who act in the belief that they can and should help to right the wrongs of South African society, but again there is no agreement about how this can be done.

Changes in the international community have had a substantial influence on Anglo/South African relations. Britain emerged from the war with an economy in tatters but a mighty empire, and in southern Africa Britain was the predominant external influence. Britain's status as a world power gave it global military and economic interests which touched South Africa. The British navy paraded the southern oceans, using Simonstown as an important base; and, on the economic side, as Britain struggled to support the sterling area and to achieve a satisfactory balance of payments, South African gold and trade played an important part. There were also the formal constitutional responsibilities of empire, with Britain's sovereignty spread across southern Africa in its colonial possessions – the three central African territories of Northern and Southern Rhodesia and Nyasaland (now Zambia, Zimbabwe and Malawi), and in the three High

Commission Territories (now Botswana, Lesotho and Swaziland). These imperial responsibilities led to regular contact with South Africa, which produced friction as well as cooperation, as is illustrated by the long squabble over the future of the High Commission Territories, and, more recently, conflicting reactions to Rhodesia's UDI.

By the 1980s most of that had changed. Britain had withdrawn from empire; there were still global economic interests but the sterling area was no more, the old military alliances in the East had gone, and there was no longer a permanent British naval presence in the Indian Ocean. There have also been striking changes in the international setting of the relationship, with many international organizations becoming vehicles for opposition to South Africa. This hostility grew from the early post-war years, and by 1961 the Republic had been forced to withdraw from the Commonwealth. Its exclusion marked a narrowing of its international options and another step along the road from being a pillar of the Allied cause to being a pariah of the international community. Those who have strong links with South Africa are never allowed to forget those links. Part of the answer to the question 'Why is it that Britain gives such prominence to South Africa?' is that others insist on it. British ministers must often have wished for a quiet life in their relations with the Republic, but every meeting of the United Nations or the Commonwealth dispels such ideas. Whatever the British may want, the Third World, and especially the black African states with which Britain retains strong contacts, ensure that there is persistent criticism of the Republic and of Britain's links with it.

The criticism persists because Britain retains such wide interests in the Republic: cultural and personal ties, and economic links which merge into strategic concerns about the supply of 'vital' minerals and the defence of the Cape route. Added to these are interests in South Africa's black neighbouring states, which were forged in the colonial days and remain to form another influence on Anglo/South African relations. These interests have to be set in an international environment of persistent hostility to South Africa, and it is partly because of that, and partly because of its own relatively declining international power, that the British government has sought to change the nature of its links with Pretoria from that of a bilateral relationship to a combined Western position. Britain's involvement in South Africa, however, is still greater than that of its alliance partners, and it is correspondingly more vulnerable internationally. Indeed, for the British government, South Africa is now an issue which intrudes into the management of the Western alliance.

The international changes interact with and stimulate change inside the two countries. The shifting composition and norms of the international community, with the increasing emphasis on racial equality and the role of black states, have been mirrored, in the Republic, in the black challenge to white dominance and, in Britain, in the debate about domestic race relations and the emergence of powerful anti-apartheid groups. British responses, however, have been far from uniform. The government, while not prepared to break its ties with South Africa, has sought to put a diplomatic distance between itself and Pretoria; the anti-apartheid groups have campaigned to break all ties and to impose sanctions on the Republic; and, finally, British business and financial communities remain as deeply enmeshed as ever.

Such diversity is not really surprising in a relationship that is so controversial and involves so many people. The broad range of the links can be illustrated by the movement of people. From the early nineteenth century Britain has been the main source of white immigrants to South Africa, and since 1945 it has provided more than half of South Africa's immigrants from outside Africa, while almost the same proportion of those who left the Republic moved to Britain. Between 1946 and 1978 more than 350,000 people emigrated from Britain to South Africa, and about 100,000 moved the other way. These are substantial figures by any standards, but in the South African context they are remarkable. No other country comes near to rivalling them. In the five years 1974–8, 64 per cent of the immigrants to the Republic from outside Africa came from Britain (74,445 out of 115,687); the next main source was West Germany, with 7 per cent (7,973 people). Britain's lead was not quite so great in receiving emigrants from South Africa in the same period, but was still significant: some 44 per cent of South Africans went to Britain (31,139 out of 71,623), the next in line being Australia with 9 per cent (6,305).

The movement of people has fluctuated according to economic and political circumstances. Britain's periodic economic crises have pushed people towards the sunshine and white prosperity of South Africa, whereas political crises there – such as the Sharpeville killings in 1960 and the Soweto riots of 1976 – have reversed the flow. In Britain this movement of people has often been associated with feelings of 'kith and kin' and sympathy for the white South Africans, and many who are active in promoting links with the Republic have family, friends and business contacts in the Republic. There is, however, another side to the coin, for personal experience and links have sometimes fostered strong anti-apartheid commitments, including those in church groups and among some members of the Labour and Liberal parties. In this way, the conflicts of the Republic are projected into British politics. British emigrants to the Republic, however, have not been particularly politically minded, and the old Afrikaner nationalist fear that they would be swamped politically by British immigration has not been realized. The great bulk of immigrants have gone to South Africa for a better standard of living, not to forward reform or revolution.

A very different picture is presented by some of the South Africans who have come to Britain. Among them are exiles who are highly politicized and throw their energies into fighting apartheid from abroad. Their impact far outweighs their numbers. They are drawn from all races and include members of the banned black nationalist parties. Others operate through the British political system, but usually via pressure groups rather than the political parties, providing a leaven to many of the anti-apartheid groups.

Although the exiles have helped to make London a centre for opposition to South Africa, it is also a centre for extensive business and financial contacts. These form a network which is built from investments, trading agreements and company structures, with many major British companies operating subsidiaries in South Africa. Great controversy surrounds these contacts. Those who oppose them argue that they help to support apartheid, and these critics underline South Africa's relative unimportance in terms of total British economic activity. In contrast, the business community emphasizes that the contacts with South Africa provide vital minerals, a vigorous market and a high return on investment. Furthermore, they claim that economic growth will undermine apartheid in South Africa. Business and financial relationships are constantly changing, but over a long period they have proved strong and resilient, and have produced a familiarity and confidence that comes from working together.

As with the business world, there is constant interaction between the two governments, but in this case the warm confidence of the past has given way to a hesitant, uneasy relationship. This reflects not only the influence of the hostile international environment, but the dominance of the National Party (NP) in South Africa, the steady growth of opposition to apartheid in Britain, and the increasingly different perceptions of the international scene among leaders in the two countries. There has been no watershed in this movement from warmth to suspicion, but rather a progression of events: the election victory of the Labour Party in Britain and the National Party in South Africa, Macmillan's 'wind of change' speech, the withdrawal from the Commonwealth, the Sharpeville killings, the arms ban, Rhodesia's UDI, the death of Steve Biko, the Soweto riots. Yet ties between Britain and South Africa are too complex and diverse, and are found at too many levels of society, for the government to be able to cut them – unless it were to place opposition to South Africa at or near the top of its agenda, and there is no sign of that. Instead it retains the links but tries to keep the relationship at arm's length.

In analysing the British government's response to South Africa, one must look not only at the general lines of policy, but inside the machinery of government, in order to identify the separate influences of the political parties and departments. The government's policy is shaped both by bargaining within its own ranks and by its response to the domestic and international settings; in the case of South Africa, it has been characterized by marginal adjustments rather than bold initiatives.

It would be difficult for the government to have behaved otherwise, for the relationship with South Africa raises and exposes a conflict of deeply held moral judgements. The relationship is set apart from most other foreign policy issues by the intensity of this moral debate, which has become so enmeshed in British politics that attitudes to South Africa have become crude litmus tests of political conviction, distinguishing 'conservative', 'liberal' and 'radical' views. Each of these broad groups has had its successes and failures. The conservatives have tried, but have failed, to have areas of activity, such as sport and trade, placed outside the political arena. However, despite the persistent criticism of the anti-apartheid groups, contacts have been retained and in some cases extended. South African cricket teams may no longer tour Britain, and arms are no longer sold; but trade, investment, immigration and tourism flourish. In that sense the conservatives can claim their successes. The liberal position has also had mixed fortunes. On the success side the public debate in Britain is largely conducted in liberal terms, with widespread condemnation of apartheid, but little support for revolutionary change. Peaceful reform is most favoured and that is the position generally adopted by the government. Nevertheless, the degree of change achieved in South Africa by peaceful pressure must disappoint even the most optimistic reformer. Finally, the radicals have succeeded in politicizing virtually all contacts with the Republic – whether it be playing games, engaging in naval exercises, selling and buying goods, extracting minerals, or using the banks that operate there – but they have not succeeded in persuading the government, and even less business interests, to break the bulk of their contacts.

This study seeks to explore the British side of Anglo/South African relations. It deals with developments within South Africa only in so far as they affect British contacts. This is not to imply that the British connection is in any way a determining factor in South African development; rather, it is to recognize that Britain – in terms of both governmental and non-governmental activities – continues to play an important part in South African affairs. It would be extraordinary to believe otherwise – with Britain's large economic interests, its continuing links with neighbouring black states, the interchange of people and ideas, the diplomatic contacts and conflicts, and the high mutual awareness between the two countries. Within Britain, concern with South Africa's internal affairs becomes part of the domestic scene, passing through the prism of British political values and processes to emerge in a form which South Africans must sometimes find hard to recognize, but which has its own importance in the context of the relationship.

Why should the relationship with South Africa be so important to Britain? There is no single answer. A variety of factors are involved, many of which have been touched on: the traditional and emotional ties, the economic contacts, the strategic concerns about the Cape route and the supply of minerals, and the prominence given to South Africa in international organizations, so that even if Britain wanted to ignore the Republic, it could not. However, the vigour of the domestic debate does not suggest any wish to do so.

2 The International Setting

South Africa is the subject of world-wide concern which finds expression in settings as diverse as the United Nations and the international cricket field. Within that broad context, Britain, because of its long association with the region, is more affected by links with the Republic than any other state outside the southern African subcontinent itself. Although other Western states have become increasingly involved, they have not internalized South African problems or given them a high priority. While the USA, for instance, has a much greater potential than Britain for exerting influence in South Africa, the issue is seldom a matter of American public concern or inter-party conflict, and, although the USA faces increasing pressure from the black states to take a stronger stand against apartheid, the Americans have treated South Africa as one, and not always a particularly prominent one, among the myriad of international problems they face. The same can be said for France and West Germany (see Appendix).

As a result, Britain is exposed and vulnerable to international pressure, and the South Africa connection overspills to influence other relationships. It affects (a) North/South relations – for the Third World, and the black states in particular, are committed against apartheid and judge others on their attitude towards it; (b) East/West relations – for the communist states use Western contacts with South Africa as a pressure-point against the West; and (c) the Western alliance – for, although other Western states are increasingly caught up in South African affairs, their views do not always coincide with Britain's.

Increasingly since the Second World War there has been an international consensus against racial discrimination, but 'discrimination' has not been interpreted universally, rather as discrimination by whites against blacks, and especially white minority rule. 'Political elites in the West', wrote Hugh Tinker, '... quickly realized that open identification with South Africa could only lead to "guilt by association". They quickly learned the new rhetoric of international equality and assimilated the new word, racism, into their vocabulary. Somewhat grudgingly, they even accepted that this was synonymous with white racism.'[1]

The presumption of 'guilt by association' has put particular pressure on

Britain. Ivor Richard spoke of this when he was British ambassador at the United Nations. In this instance he was referring to Rhodesia, but his words could just as easily be applied to South Africa:

> When you get perhaps 130 out of 140 countries expressing a clear view as to what the British government should do over Rhodesia, well obviously we don't want to be isolated, particularly if we find that some of our closest partners, say in the West, or in the EEC, or in NATO, themselves have doubts and qualifications about the policy Britain is pursuing. And while you could possibly ignore the Warsaw Pact powers as being biased in one direction, when you get a line-up of all the African countries, all the other non-aligned countries, Asian countries, some of the Western countries, the Scandinavian countries, and you get that line-up on the other side of the argument to Great Britain, well obviously . . . it makes you think as to why you find yourself in this position and what you can do to avoid it.[2]

Richard's statement underlines both the strength of international opposition to white racism and Britain's cross-cutting concerns – the fear of isolation from Western allies, and the suspicions of the Warsaw Pact powers 'as being biased in one direction'.

In all Britain's dealings with South Africa, the advantages of retaining links have to be balanced against the disadvantages. This is particularly true of the East/West security issue. If Britain's main aim is to strengthen the West's military forces against the threat of Soviet expansion, then there are strong grounds for working closely with South Africa. The Republic is firmly anti-communist; it has important bases and facilities (such as the naval base at Simonstown, and the communications and surveillance centre at Silvermine); it provides a regular flow of minerals to the West; and its armed forces are probably the most efficient in Africa. Yet no Western state is likely to endanger its international reputation by entering into a formal alliance with the Republic. Those who may favour closer military links accept that any cooperation has to be covert – an unsatisfactory situation for both sides because of its high potential for misunderstanding. (This was well illustrated when the South Africans intervened in Angola in 1976, believing that they had American support, whereas the Americans backed out, leaving the South Africans exposed. The bitterness that resulted helps to explain South Africa's later suspicions of the West during the Namibia negotiations.)

On the other hand, Britain, and other Western states, although they have tried to distance themselves from South Africa diplomatically, have never been prepared to commit themselves to the 'liberation struggle'. They have offered substantial economic, and some military, aid to black states, but not to the southern African liberation movements or their armies. In contrast, the communist states have given little aid to black Africa, but they have provided military support for the liberation movements, and that, together with the fact that they are not smeared by association with the Republic, has enhanced their prestige in black Africa at the expense of the West.

The Commonwealth

There are three international organizations through which the black states have brought pressure to bear on Britain: the Commonwealth, the United Nations and the Organization of African Unity (OAU). The international difficulties created for Britain by the South Africa connection are nowhere more clearly illustrated than in the Commonwealth. To examine these involves looking briefly at the past, and paying attention to the problems of white minority rule in southern Africa generally.

For many post-war British leaders, the Commonwealth held out glittering prizes. It was to give Britain a continuing role as a major power with a spread of interests and responsibilities across the globe. Its claims to be anything more than a European power rested on that vision. However, the Commonwealth countries did not have common interests and values, nor did Britain have the resources to sustain a global role. Gradually over the 1960s and 1970s British policy-makers came to terms with this, but the process was slow, and in the case of southern Africa it was painful and damaging to Britain's international position.

The Commonwealth conferences of this period were dominated by southern African problems, and two of them were directly related to South Africa: first, its application for renewed membership of the organization, and, second, the sale of arms. The dispute over membership came to a head in 1961 following the declaration – in May of that year – of a Republic in South Africa. Since there were already several republican members, this in itself need not have caused problems, and Harold Macmillan, who chaired the conference, favoured readmitting South Africa. However, criticism of South Africa's racial policies was so fierce that a direct clash between Britain and the black states was avoided only because Dr Verwoerd, the South African prime minister, withdrew the application for renewed membership. Verwoerd said that his decision was not only in South Africa's interests but in those of 'our friends in the Commonwealth, particularly the United Kingdom. I could not place them in the invidious position of having to choose between South Africa and a group of Afro-Asian states'.[3]

Although the membership crisis was overcome, Commonwealth divisions over white minority rule were equally clear when South Africa next dominated the agenda – with the dispute about arms sales at the Singapore Conference in 1971. Before the conference opened, President Kaunda of Zambia had warned that the decision of the new British Conservative government of Edward Heath to sell arms for 'external' use 'would be an act of aggression against human rights and would be the worst example of a government that believes in peace and professes respect for human rights. There can be no excuse on their part for resuming the sale of arms to South Africa and ignoring completely the United Nations Resolution on this issue.'[4] It was in these terms that Heath was attacked at the conference, and found himself isolated even from the old white Commonwealth members.

The bitterness against Heath in 1971 was all the greater because by then the British had failed to settle the Rhodesian problem. This had arisen in 1965, following the unilateral declaration of independence by the Smith regime in an attempt to perpetuate white minority rule. With the not uncritical support of South Africa, the Rhodesians survived for fifteen years. In the long days of that crisis, the Commonwealth conferences became arenas for British humiliation, not prestige, and year by year the British steadily abandoned their earlier Commonwealth dreams, to accept a more limited European role.

More recently, South Africa has featured in another Commonwealth dispute, this time about sporting links. The dispute flared up at the 1977 conference when the African states which had boycotted the Olympic Games in the previous year, because of New Zealand's sports links with the Republic, threatened to do the same to the 1978 Commonwealth Games. However, an agreement was reached at informal talks held during a weekend break from the conference at the Gleneagles Hotel. After reaffirming support for the international campaign against apartheid, and recognizing that sporting links could encourage a belief that apartheid was condoned, each government agreed 'to combat the evil of apartheid by withholding any form of support for, and by taking every practical step to discourage, contact or competition by their nationals with sporting organizations, teams or sportsmen from South Africa'. However, the agreement went on to acknowledge that 'it was for each government to determine in accordance with its laws, the methods by which it might best discharge its commitment'.[5]

The Gleneagles Agreement has been only a partial success, for, despite the efforts to paper over the cracks, there are differences of commitment and political culture which affect attitudes to sports links. The black states believe that Commonwealth governments should ban all sporting links, whereas governments like those in Britain and New Zealand (and especially when conservative administrations are in power) are prepared to express their opposition, but they emphasize that the sporting bodies are private organizations and in the end have to make up their own minds. However, the international pressure has been so strong that even Mrs Thatcher's administration has tried vigorously through Neil Macfarlane, the Minister of Sport, to persuade bodies like the Rugby Union to break their ties with South Africa.

Ironically, after all the disputes, the Commonwealth played an important part in reaching a Rhodesian settlement. Such an outcome looked unlikely when the Thatcher government came to power in 1979, announcing its hopes of reaching a settlement with the mixed-race Rhodesia/Zimbabwe government of Ian Smith and Bishop Muzorewa. This was completely rejected by the black states, and the new British government soon came to accept that the problem could be settled only by international agreement. The foundations for that agreement were laid at the Commonwealth Conference in Lusaka in August 1979. There Mrs Thatcher and Lord Carrington surprised their critics, and perhaps even themselves, by recruiting the support of the whole Commonwealth for a new British initiative.

This was a critical change. Instead of Britain finding itself alone, or at best working with the old white Commonwealth, it now had the support of its severest critics – the neighbouring black states, which were patrons of the Patriotic Front forces. These states were eager to bring an end to a costly and bloody war into which they had increasingly been drawn, and from their side of the battle lines the South Africans felt the same. They, too, wanted a negotiated end to the running sore of the Rhodesian war, and were prepared to use their not inconsiderable influence with Smith and Muzorewa to achieve it. The international dimension was very clear in the negotiations. The settlement reached at Lancaster House, with Lord Carrington presiding over the Zimbabwe parties, was achieved only with supporting pressure from the neighbouring states on their clients – including South African pressure on Smith and Muzorewa. Without that, and without the fatigue of war, the British could not have steered the way to a settlement; on the other hand, the British government exploited the opportunity with great diplomatic skill and improved its international reputation in the process.

Two further points need to be made. First, the Rhodesian crisis underlines the centrality of South Africa's role in the subcontinent. When Britain had colonial responsibilities in southern Africa, it was drawn into a working relationship with the Republic, whether in connection with the High Commission Territories, or the Central African Federation, or later Rhodesia. Despite an element of distrust on both sides, the British and the South Africans looked to each other to find a Rhodesian settlement. There were several joint initiatives, bringing together such unlikely characters as David Owen and John Vorster into a timid working relationship. Second, too much should not be read into Britain's eventual success over Rhodesia. Britain's approach to southern African affairs is to search for compromise and incremental change, but this has often appeared weak and irrelevant in a situation of confrontation. In the Rhodesia case it was only when the cost of continuing the struggle became too great for those directly involved that Britain's diplomatic and compromise approach became effective. That situation certainly does not exist in South Africa at present, and therefore the tension within British relations will continue.

The United Nations

At the United Nations, as in the Commonwealth, Britain regularly has to make fine judgements in balancing its interests in retaining links with South Africa against the persistent criticism and pressures of the black states backed by the Eastern bloc. The campaign against the Republic at the United Nations can be categorized in three ways: first, opposition to internal racial policies; second, the claim that South Africa is a threat to international peace; and, third, accusations that it has acted illegally in Namibia.

The core issue is the first of these – racial discrimination. The others stem from that. This was true even in the first limited UN attacks, which were led by India and concentrated on the treatment of the Asians of South Africa. As the black states gained independence, the range and intensity of the attacks grew, to cover discrimination against all the blacks. Also the nature of the attacks changed from concern about individual rights in a particular state to a universal attack upon racial inequality, and from attempts to pressure or persuade the South African government to change its policies to a commitment to overthrowing the existing racial structure of the society.

In their attempts to persuade others, and especially the Western states, to take action, the black states have persistently argued that South Africa is a threat to international peace. Although they genuinely believe that racial inequality is the greatest threat to future world peace and order (and brush aside the South African accusation that they are themselves the source of the threat in southern Africa by their interference in the affairs of the sovereign state of South Africa), this is not a view shared by the Western governments. Debates at the UN have therefore often turned on the apparent technicality of whether or not South Africa is a threat to international peace, but behind the technicality is the critical issue that if South Africa is so designated, mandatory action could be ordered by the Security Council, overriding the sovereign rights of the Republic.

In the case of Namibia, one of the tactics of the black states has been to use legal channels as a source of pressure – conscious that states like Britain pride themselves on upholding the law. They have not met with much success. Namibia (or South West Africa) was a German colony which was put under South African control at the end of the First World War as one of the League of Nations' mandated territories. Since the end of the Second World War there have been endless legal-cum-diplomatic disputes about its status and future. For the black states its release from South African control forms part of the overall campaign against racism, and they have sought legal means to try to achieve this, but while the slow and sometimes ambiguous judgements handed down by the International Court of Justice took some of the pressure off the West, they only created frustration among the Afro-Asian states.

Yet despite the relative failure of the legalistic approach, the black states have used the international agencies to considerable effect. First, they are focal points of the anti-apartheid effort, whether it be in the UN General Assembly, where the majority vote has been so effective, or at the OAU, where opposition to apartheid has been a unifying factor among diversity. Second, they have become instruments in reshaping international attitudes. The changes in the British government's position illustrate this. In the immediate post-war years the British, although urging the South Africans to modify their racial policies, argued that South Africa's internal policies were not a direct UN concern and therefore lay outside the competence of the organization. Step by step that position was eroded, and often the steps were linked to black protests at internal troubles in the Republic. Following the Sharpeville massacre in 1960, the British recognized apartheid as a matter of international concern and openly started to voice their criticism. Later they came to accept the arms bans against the Republic, notably the UN's mandatory ban of 1977 which followed the Soweto riots and the death of Steve Biko. The third function of the international organizations has been to legitimize the campaign against apartheid. Much of the anti-apartheid work has been done by non-governmental groups, which have been given an authority and a legitimacy by the UN General Assembly and the UN Special Committee on Apartheid, which was formed in 1962. The Special Committee, using the work of the groups, has often taken the initiative against South Africa, setting up hearings, promoting studies, providing a full-time secretariat to service the campaign, and issuing propaganda.

The case of Robin Jackman, the English cricketer, illustrates the links involved. Early in 1981 Jackman was called as a replacement for another English cricketer in the West Indies. As Jackman was preparing to join the team, it became known that he was on a UN black list of sportsmen who had played in South Africa. On the basis of these reports, the Guyana government, where the team was staying at the time, refused Jackman entry, a test match was called off, the English cricketers moved on without playing in Guyana, and for a while it looked as though the whole tour would be cancelled. In Britain, the debate was reopened about contacts with South Africa, the right of individuals to decide whether or not they played, the evils of apartheid, and so on. This international incident had been triggered off by the work of a small anti-apartheid group, the South

African Non-Racial Olympic Committee (SANROC), which had drawn up a list of British sportsmen who had regularly visited South Africa. The list received the approval of the UN Special Committee, which called on governments and sports organizations to refuse to allow those named to compete in international events. Jackman's case is therefore something of a classic. The anti-apartheid group SANROC did the initial work, the UN Special Committee legitimized and gave authority to that work, the Guyana government (although under no compulsion to act) decided to implement it, and a great stir was caused in Britain, with the media giving the incident heavy publicity.

Exclusion tactics have also been used regularly against the South African government and other South African organizations. The example established at the Commonwealth Conference in 1961 was followed by a series of expulsions and attempted expulsions. Generally the British have opposed these, arguing the principle of universality, whereby the strength of international organizations, and especially the United Nations, rests on the inclusion of states whatever their political complexion. Once that is abandoned, so this argument goes, the effectiveness of the UN and its agencies is greatly diminished, and also there will be endless disputes about who can and cannot have membership. British governments have shared the sentiments of the US ambassador at the UN who, in vetoing the call for South Africa's exclusion in 1974, said that expulsion 'could gravely damage the UN structure. It would bring into question one of the fundamental concepts on which the Charter is based – the concept of a forum in which ideas and ideals are voiced along with conflicting views.'[6]

However, the Western opposition to exclusion has been largely unsuccessful, and this has included a number of UN agencies. The World Health Organization (WHO) provides an example. At a meeting of the WHO's African regional group in the autumn of 1963, there was a direct confrontation between the black states, demanding South Africa's expulsion, and the South Africans, backed by Britain and France, who enjoyed membership of the regional group because of their colonial possessions. The black states refused to attend if the South Africans were present, and it became clear that it was a choice of abandoning the organization or South Africa's membership of it. In the following year this situation was resolved when South Africa withdrew – after a vote for its exclusion had been carried by 66 votes in favour to 6 against (including Britain) and 23 abstentions.

In 1971 the General Assembly, by a majority vote, with Britain and other Western states opposing, decided to reject the credentials of the South African delegates because they did not represent the people of that country. In 1974 there was a further attempt to exclude South Africa completely from the UN, but that was vetoed in the Security Council by

Britain, France and the USA. For Britain, Ivor Richard said that the objective should be not to purge the UN but to persuade South Africa to change its policies. However, the General Assembly has continued to reject South Africa's credentials, declaring that the representation should be vested in the African liberation movements, so that the Republic retains the status of a UN member but plays little part in its formal activities.

The black states had a significant victory in 1977 when they persuaded the Security Council to impose a mandatory arms ban against South Africa, but they have not succeeded in their main ambition: to have the Security Council impose mandatory economic sanctions against the Republic. As with the membership issue, this has faltered on Western vetoes. The campaign for economic sanctions has been a persistent one, stretching back to the 1960s. In 1964 a London conference called by anti-apartheid groups, and attracting the heads of several African states, gave a boost to the sanctions campaign by concluding that sanctions were 'necessary, urgent, legal and practical'. There was, however, one great proviso. Sanctions, said the conference report, were likely to succeed only 'with the full cooperation of Britain and the United States'.[7]

That degree of cooperation has never been forthcoming, even when the British were in such trouble over their Rhodesia policy. In this instance it was the British themselves who had called on the UN to apply economic sanctions against the erring colony. Harold Wilson had personally committed himself to make them effective, and the British government had a considerable stake in their implementation, but they did not succeed – mainly because South Africa continued to offer full trading and financial facilities to the Rhodesians. In this case Britain had a strong motive to take action against the Republic. It did not. The price of an economic war against South Africa was thought to be too high, as George Thomson, one of the ministers involved, later explained: 'We came increasingly to the conclusion... that we couldn't bring the Rhodesian Government to an end by sanctions, unless we were prepared to apply them to South Africa. We were under no circumstances willing to do that.'[8]

Britain and the other Western states see themselves caught in the middle of the South African dispute at international organizations. While the South Africans complain that the West kowtows to black pressure, the black states believe that the West acts as a shield to protect the South Africans against the full fury of international reaction. From the black viewpoint, the West has, first, sought to keep South Africa within the international community; second, tried to modify the attacks against it; and, third, refused to support the liberation movement despite strong backing for it at the UN. In 1977 Sir David Scott, the British ambassador to South Africa, told a South African audience that the four most recent vetoes Britain had been forced to cast at the Security Council had been to protect South Africa. With regard to Britain's position at international organizations, he said: 'We now find ourselves with little ammunition left to defend ourselves against intense international criticism that we are leaning over backwards to defend South Africa's internal policies'.[9]

At the United Nations the black states, recognizing their limitations, have set mandatory economic sanctions as their objective, but elsewhere they have supported the armed struggle. In particular the Organization of African Unity has helped to legitimize the liberation movements and give them an international status. An OAU Liberation Committee was set up to give material aid to the black nationalist fighters in southern Africa, but overall the performance of the committee has been inept – partly owing to its own divisions and inefficiency, and partly because the separate black governments have not provided the material support they promised.

The liberation movements have gained rather more effective, although not military, support from some of the UN agencies – notably the United Nations High Commission for Refugees (UNHCR) and the United Nations Education, Scientific and Cultural Organization (UNESCO). UNHCR became involved through helping people driven from their homes in the southern African fighting – in the old Portuguese territories and Rhodesia – and in the same way UNESCO started to offer educational facilities to the refugees. Subsequently UNESCO interpreted its role more widely, as part of the liberation struggle, and became a source of support for the OAU, especially after the appointment of a full-time UNESCO representative to the OAU in 1970.

It is perhaps appropriate that UNESCO has become so involved in southern Africa, because it is in a broad educational role that the international organizations have played their most effective part. The black states looked to the organizations for quick, sharp, dramatic action; yet, for all the noise, all the rhetoric, the resolutions, conferences and threats, that has not been achieved. The international organizations have proved to be neither sharp nor flexible instruments. Instead they have, albeit unintentionally, taken on an educational role, changing the international agenda in a way that was neither foreseen nor particularly welcomed by Britain and the other Western states. Slowly but steadily international attitudes to racial discrimination have changed; slowly but steadily the white rulers of South Africa have been isolated; slowly but steadily the cause of the black nationalists has been legitimized. As far as the British are concerned, they have followed in the wake of this, as they have come to accept that the racial policies of the South African government are matters for international concern and action.

The black states

Black opposition to South Africa has intruded into direct interstate relations, in which Britain has been vulnerable because of its continuing links and its colonial past. This is illustrated by Britain's relations with the Front Line states – a group of black states whose common interests and problems arise from bordering on the war zones against the white rulers. At first the conflicts were in Mozambique, Angola and Rhodesia, but as these states were 'liberated', so they joined the group, as the 'front line' moved to Namibia and South Africa itself. The Front Line states have both supported the guerrillas and engaged in the international negotiations associated with the disputes, and it is this that has brought them into regular contact with the British government. They were actively involved in the Rhodesian conflict and the Zimbabwe settlement, and, now that international attention has turned more sharply to the struggles in Namibia and South Africa, they have again become the virtual representatives of all black Africa, without which an acceptable international settlement cannot be found.

The main participants in the Namibia dispute – the South African government and the internal parties (the South West Africa People's Organization (SWAPO), which is favoured by the black states, and the Democratic Turnhalle Alliance (DTA), which has South African support) – are joined both by the Front Line states and by the Western 'Contact Group'. This group, which consists of Britain, the USA, West Germany, France and Canada, was formed in 1977 when the five Western members who were serving on the Security Council at the time that the Namibia problem surfaced again started to coordinate their efforts in *ad hoc* meetings. It has hung together ever since. The Five see themselves as a channel of communication and advice – honest brokers between the protagonists – but this view is not necessarily shared by the protagonists themselves. The black states believe that the group has often acted to defend South Africa from the wrath of the international community, while the South Africans believe that the Western states are concerned, not with gaining a just solution, but with defending their own international positions, which often means giving way to the extreme demands of the black majority at the United Nations. For the South Africans, the very fact that the group is trying to work through the UN gives further ground for distrust because they believe that the UN is deeply biased against them. In this situation the role of honest broker is especially difficult and can succeed only if the interests of the diverse parties to the dispute happen to coincide in wanting a settlement.

The impact of Britain's connections with South Africa extends outside southern Africa, across the whole continent. Frequently critics of white South Africa present the situation in terms of a direct choice – between

South Africa and black Africa. They argue that – not only on moral grounds but in terms of material interests – Britain is best served in siding with the black states, for time is on their side, and already the size of Britain's trade with black Africa is much greater than that with the Republic. The British have refused to see the situation in these terms. Their aim has been to retain advantageous contacts with both sides. Nevertheless, whenever this option is raised, worried British eyes turn to Nigeria, the largest and richest of the black states. The British stake in Nigeria is large. According to a *Financial Times* supplement of 29 September 1980, Britain held 50 per cent of the total book assets of external investment in Nigeria based on 1977 figures. British trade with Nigeria showed a healthy surplus, and by 1980 Nigeria was spending twice as much on British goods as South Africa – having become Britain's largest market outside Europe and the USA.

From the British viewpoint the Nigerian danger is threefold: first, that Nigeria may use its leading position in Africa to organize a coordinated campaign against Britain; second, that it will try to exert indirect pressure on Britain by the influence it now enjoys in other Western states; and, third, that the Nigerians will take direct action against British interests in Nigeria itself. There appeared to be little danger of these before the over-throw of General Gowon in 1975. Until then Nigeria had followed a 'moderate' policy towards the Republic. However, a new government under General Murtala Muhammad, building on the confidence which came from the country's increasing oil wealth and its recovery from the bloody civil war, adopted a much clearer leadership role in black Africa and in doing so committed itself against South Africa. The first clear display of this came in Nigeria's reaction against South African involve-ment in the Angolan civil war, and the opposition has persisted, despite the subsequent changes in the government.

Nigeria's leading position in Africa has been demonstrated in the number of its important visitors, and the Nigerians have not lost the opportunity on such occasions to reaffirm their opposition to apartheid, and to explain the action they are prepared to take. One potential source of Nigerian pressure on Britain is via the USA. The Americans have given increased attention to Nigeria because of its leadership role in Africa, and also because of America's increased economic links, especially Nigeria's oil supplies. When President Obasanjo visited the USA in 1977, President Carter greeted him by describing Nigeria as undoubtedly the most important country economically in Africa. In reply, Obasanjo introduced the subject of apartheid, saying that it was 'a crime that not only Africa but all mankind must fight'.[10] Three years later, when President Shagari visited the USA, he even suggested that Nigeria might use the oil weapon to pressure the USA into opposition of South Africa. Although the chances of Nigeria influencing US policy seems less likely with the advent of the Reagan administration, the economic links remain and the possibility of future Nigerian pressure on Britain's Western allies cannot be discounted.

In its direct contacts with Britain, Nigeria has gone further than threats on two occasions. The first followed the news in December 1976 that Barclays Bank in the Republic had purchased South African government bonds which were to help finance the war effort against the black nationalist guerrillas. The Nigerian response was to withdraw all its deposits from Barclays and to order two-thirds of the expatriate staff to be withdrawn. The Nigerian decision seems to have been prompted directly by the action of the British bank, but there may also have been anger at Britain for harbouring ex-President Gowon, who was accused in Nigeria of trying to organize a coup.

The second action came in August 1979. As the Commonwealth leaders were assembling for the Lusaka Conference, the news broke that the Nigerian government had nationalized BP's assets and that a blanket prohibition had been placed on British companies tendering for Nigerian government contracts. These were considerable blows, for BP was staggering under the recent loss of the Iranian fields, and at that time was drawing about 10 per cent of its total world supplies from Nigeria. The reason given by the Nigerians was that a tanker which had been chartered by BP, and which had called at Lagos, was South Africa-owned. In an angry exchange at the start of the Lusaka Conference, Lord Carrington accused the Nigerians of taking action that had nothing to do with BP, but was a crude attempt to pressure the British government into changing its Rhodesia policy before it had even been discussed at the conference. Ironically, the Lusaka Conference led to the eventual Rhodesian settlement and Zimbabwe's independence. Following that, Anglo-Nigerian relations were gradually repaired, but the potential dangers had been amply demonstrated. Equally, however, the British government and business community are aware of limitations on Nigeria's power. Although Nigeria aspires to be the leader of black Africa, it has not been able to consolidate that position among a group of states that have been united against South Africa but divided on many other issues. Moreover, Nigeria has suffered from internal political divisions, and these, together with substantial fluctuations in the country's trade, and problems of inefficiency and corruption, have combined not only to undermine its leadership claim but to create an uncertain business climate inside the country.

Western partners
In the difficult international setting that surrounds South Africa, it is

increasingly in Britain's interests to work closely with its Western partners – to find safety in the pack. Until the 1960s, Britain was the major external power in southern Africa, while the superpowers had given the subcontinent relatively little attention. During the 1970s that position began to change. East European states gained an increasing foothold through their support for the liberation movements, and Western states, including the USA, increased their economic and security interests. The involvement of the other Western states has the advantages for Britain of promoting common perceptions and spreading the burden of association with the Republic, but there are strains. Some of the smaller Western states, such as the Scandinavian countries and the Netherlands, have taken a radical stance towards South Africa and have given non-military aid to the liberation movements, perhaps because they have relatively little at stake in the Republic. Those who have more at stake, such as Britain, the USA, France and West Germany, take a more cautious approach. Since this group contains the largest and richest of the Western states, as well as three permanent members of the UN Security Council, its views will be taken to represent 'the West' in general. Yet even when policy considerations are confined to these four countries, the problem of alliance management for Britain remains.

For the Western governments, southern Africa presents a mixed picture of common interests and potential divisions. The common features stretch across strategic and economic interests, concern with the stability of the subcontinent and more generally the international system as a whole. The potential divisions include economic rivalry, different degrees of reliance upon South Africa and the neighbouring states, different perceptions of the strategic importance of southern Africa, and the different domestic bases from which the governments operate. On the one hand, therefore, it is in Britain's interest that the Western states work closely together, but on the other hand the attempt to cooperate raises tensions, and, unless the government manages the situation well, Britain's special interests could isolate it from its partners and reduce its general international influence.

The strains are often revealed by particular events rather than general pronouncements. For example, in the Angola crisis of 1975–6 there were differences between the Americans and the members of the European Community, and differences within the Community. The hopes of a united EC response were thwarted when the French gave unilateral recognition to the MPLA government of President Neto. Similarly, the USA failed to keep the European states informed of its actions and decisions. Moreover, while the US administration tended to see the situation largely in East/West terms, the British and French, with long-standing African interests and experience, saw it more in continental terms – in its impact on relations between the black states, and between them and the West.

The division was even sharper in the Western response to the South African invasion of Angola in August 1981 – an operation which the South Africans claimed was part of the war they were waging with the SWAPO guerrillas who were infiltrating into Namibia, whereas the Angolan government saw it as a direct attack on its sovereign territory. When the invasion was brought before the UN Security Council, the West was in disarray, with the three permanent members voting in different ways – the French supporting a motion condemning the South Africans, the USA vetoing it, and the British abstaining. The conflicting views of the Americans and the French are partly explained by changes in their governments, with a right-wing administration taking office in the USA and a socialist one in France. Britain's vote at the UN was therefore cast with only half an eye on Angola; equally important was the need to restore Western unity, and in those terms the British saw their abstention not as a negative act but as the first step in rebuilding Western bridges.

More generally, American involvement in southern Africa illustrates the problems for Britain of reconciling its own interests and policies with those of its Western partners. Until the 1970s the USA played a relatively small role in the subcontinent. It entered the scene for a number of reasons: the spread of East/West tensions into Africa, the increasing importance of black Africa in international organizations, growing domestic concern with racial matters, and the increase in American business activity and investment in South Africa. But there is no deep-rooted American experience of southern Africa on which a consistent response has been built. Instead, the Americans have been tempted to see the region in terms of 'great causes' – whether it be in defence of 'the free world' or in forwarding human rights – and to symbolize their policies by bold gestures. They have thereby oversimplified the region's problems, and have produced volatile policies reflecting the changing perceptions and ideological commitments of different administrations.

In 1969 President Nixon and Secretary of State Henry Kissinger asked the US National Security Council to report on American interests in southern Africa. When the report was submitted it was based on the assumption that for many years to come white rule was secure – including the Portuguese territories and Rhodesia. Moreover, it concluded that although southern Africa affected a range of American interests, 'none of the interests are vital to our security but they have political and material importance'.[11] By the mid-1970s the report's assumption about white control had fallen apart with the collapse of the Portuguese empire and the increased intensity of the struggle in Rhodesia.

It was the instability caused by the fall of the Portuguese colonies that drew Henry Kissinger directly onto the scene. He brought to southern Africa his distinctive style of trade-offs, package deals, pressure politics and shuttle diplomacy. His aim was to manage the international system to achieve global détente and balance, which, among other things, implied avoiding regional conflicts that might threaten the whole system. In southern Africa his first effort was to try to counter communist influence in Angola by giving covert support to the South Africans, and by backing the movements inside Angola which were opposed to the Soviet-backed MPLA (People's Movement for the Liberation of Angola). That failed. Even at home Congress refused to back his policies, and in Angola itself the MPLA, with the support of Cuban troops, succeeded in forming a government.

Kissinger's second major effort – an attempt to find a Rhodesian settlement – paid greater regard to black views. He sought to pressure all parties to seek a settlement, and persuaded the South Africans to use their power to influence the white Rhodesians. Despite South African bitterness at the American 'betrayal' in Angola, they were sufficiently eager to gain a Rhodesian settlement that they backed Kissinger's efforts. For the first time Smith was forced to accept in public the principle of majority rule. The British worked so closely with Kissinger that he used British briefing papers in the negotiations, and the British took over responsibility again when a constitutional conference was called at Geneva to try to gain the agreement of all parties to the new proposals.[12] There, however, the early hopes were dashed, for the concessions that Smith was prepared to make were far removed from the claims of the black nationalists. By the time that became clear, the Republicans – including Dr Kissinger – had been replaced by President Jimmy Carter's Democrats.

The new administration took an immediate interest in southern Africa, but the whole tenor of American policy changed. Attempts to manage the international system gave way to concern for individual human rights, and the search for a balance of power was replaced by a moral crusade. Walter Mondale, the new vice-president, antagonized John Vorster, the South African prime minister, by telling him that America was committed to the principle of black majority rule in the Republic. British involvement with this new wave of American policy was again mainly linked to Rhodesia. David Owen, the British foreign secretary, and Andy Young, the American ambassador to the UN, worked closely together to produce an Anglo-American proposal for a settlement. Yet, as with previous attempts, it failed – in this case partly because of the whites' distrust of Owen and Young. Then, like much else in the Carter presidency, the early southern African initiatives ran into the sands.

When Reagan's administration replaced Carter's, it had little experience in foreign policy. Nevertheless, its broad orientation was clear: it was a right-wing government whose world view was dominated by the East/West conflict. Within that picture, the USA saw itself leading the fight to defend capitalist enterprise and political freedom from communism, and this led to greater sympathy for the anti-communist white government of South Africa. After some vacillation, the administration's policy towards southern Africa began to take shape. It was one of 'constructive contact'. In August 1981, in a statement cleared 'at the highest authority', Dr Chester Crocker, the Assistant Secretary of State for African Affairs (with echoes of the early Kissinger), said that the USA did not see its task as choosing between black and white; rather, its aim was to build democratic systems which would be strong economically and counter the spread of communism. The American government had 'no intention of destabilizing South Africa in order to curry favour elsewhere. Neither will we align ourselves with apartheid policies that are abhorrent to our own multiracial democracy.' The USA recognized the importance of its own economic interests in the region, and also that there was a danger that it could become 'a cockpit of mounting East/West tension'. Crocker concluded that the easy way forward was by peaceful reform.[13]

The Americans saw this as an 'even-handed' policy, but it did not appear that way to the black states – especially since it came at a time when the Americans were helping the South Africans at the UN by vetoing the resolution condemning the invasion of Angola. Since the black states can see no middle ground in the struggle against South Africa, the actions and sentiments of the Americans were interpreted as direct support for the white racists.

Yet, despite the vacillations that have surrounded US policy, all British governments have encouraged American involvement in southern Africa. There are obvious advantages in harnessing American influence and power, and in sharing the burdens of a difficult, controversial region. Furthermore, in recent years government attitudes in the two countries have broadly coincided, so that David Owen and Andy Young were able to work together in trying to pressure the whites into reform and threatening sanctions if there was no response, while Margaret Thatcher's election victory in Britain was soon followed by that of the equally conservative Ronald Reagan in the USA. Such close coincidence of perception and interest may not persist, but what is clear is that, for Britain, relations with South Africa can no longer be seen predominantly in bilateral terms; they are firmly caught up in its relations with other Western states.

3 The Economic Stake

There is a complex web of economic relations between Britain and South Africa – of trade, banking, mining, insurance, investment, the provision of markets, the transfer of skilled manpower and technology. Within the web is a dynamic relationship, which, although constantly changing in response to domestic and international developments, has so far shown great resilience. Its size and strength are recognized on all sides, and indeed some of South Africa's bitterest opponents are the first to underline the power and pervasiveness of the relationship. As one study points out, 'There can scarcely be a single pension fund, insurance company, building society or unit trust in Britain that does not have some of its capital invested in South Africa. Students, trade unionists or clergymen who complain that their university, union or church funds are making unwholesome profit out of a racialist society have only come across a small crack in the ground beneath their feet'.[1] Both the anti-apartheid critics and the business community recognize the size and profitability of the economic links, but there is no further agreement. While one side condemns the links as a means of reinforcing apartheid and says that Britain could easily manage without them, the other applauds them as a vital contribution to Britain's economic well-being and – in South Africa – as a way of breaking down apartheid by opening up economic opportunities for the blacks.

The extent and degree of its economic involvement with South Africa have caused increasing concern in Britain. This is due to two factors: uncertainty about South Africa's internal stability, and international and domestic pressures against the Republic. British voices are heard calling for a reduction in the economic stake in South Africa, because, apart from any moral questions, it leaves the country exposed and vulnerable. The danger of internal instability carries with it the fear that British markets, supplies and investments will be lost either in the chaos following a breakdown of order, or through the triumph of a government opposed to Western capitalism, or through a mixture of the two. In its international relations, the size of the economic stake has imposed constraints on Britain, and has sometimes isolated it even from Western allies who are less dependent on the Republic. Yet, because of the high priority on economic ends, no British government has been prepared to break the ties, and if they are to be retained there is advantage for the British in other Western states increasing their stake in the Republic so that interests and perceptions will be more widely shared.

Part of the uncertainty on the British side is whether the economic links with South Africa can be judged in their own right or whether they must be measured against economic interests elsewhere. To put it bluntly, is there an economic choice between black Africa and the Republic? Even the chief executive of UKSATA (United Kingdom–South Africa Trade Association), speaking in a personal capacity in February 1981, had to recognize the dilemma: 'The importance of British trade with South Africa is self-evident from the gross earnings, the visible trade amounting to just over £1,000m. This, however, compares with visible trade to OAU countries valued for 1980 at £3,284m. British imports from South Africa for 1980 totalled £756m against imports from the OAU countries of £1,753m. British companies are being pushed into choices from which there is no easy escape'.[2]

Those who argue that a blunt choice has to be made believe that the future lies with the black Africans, for not only do they already outdistance the Republic in terms of trade with Britain but the gap is increasing. According to this view, it is short-sighted to retain the strong South Africa connection. Others, however, argue that no such choice has to be made, and that Britain's best bet is to keep open as many economic links as possible. Moreover, if Britain were to decide its economic links on moral grounds, with whom would it be trading? According to this view, there is also no evidence to suggest that the black states would take concerted action against Britain, partly because it would be so difficult to organize and partly because it would adversely affect their own interests. Finally in this argument, and looking to the future, past behaviour in Africa indicates that, whatever the political or racial composition of the government, the economic rewards go to those who are on the spot and have retained their links during the political changes. The message from that is to hang on wherever you can.

Another area of uncertainty and controversy is the strength of the South African economy, and how it responds to broader economic and political developments. One of the most striking features of the bilateral relationship has been Britain's relative decline in economic wealth and power, whereas the South African economy has been more volatile. If, in health terms, Britain has suffered from a chronic debilitating disease, South Africa appears to have enjoyed vigorous good health, interposed with periods of high fever. The fevers have usually followed political upheavals such as Sharpeville in 1960 and the Soweto riots of 1976, when confidence drained away from the Republic. Following the Soweto riots, even the high interest rates that South Africa has been able to offer were not enough to satisfy the international financial community. In 1977 the managing director of Barclays Bank in South Africa returned empty-handed from London after failing to raise two small loans. He explained that British and American banks were not prepared to expose themselves after the recent disturbances and South Africa's poor balance-of-payments situation.[3]

In the 1975–7 period the South African economy was in trouble not only from political problems but as a result of the world economic recession. Real incomes were falling, unemployment was rising for all races, output was stagnant, inflation was high, and there was the balance-of-payments problem. Yet the South African economy has also had long periods of sustained growth, and has shown the ability to recover from crises. In the case of investments, for example, the gloom of 1977 was soon replaced with confidence. By January 1979 Barclays Bank in Johannesburg could confidently say that there was no difficulty in raising foreign loans for up to five years.[4] In 1980 the South African government floated a large Eurobond, and obtained an international syndicated credit, probably as much to show the country's confidence and ability to raise international support as for any pressing need for outside capital. With employment and disposable incomes rising, production and company profitability increasing, and gold booming, such a response was readily forthcoming.

These contrasts point up a debate among Western economists about the nature of the South African economy. In broad terms, one group sees it as a windfall economy, which has so far progressed through a series of chance developments – mineral finds, the influx of skilled white labour from elsewhere in Africa, the benefits that were derived from Rhodesia's UDI, gold bonanzas, and so on. According to this view the windfalls do not create a pattern and therefore cannot be relied upon for the future, particularly with so much political uncertainty. The other group maintains that all economies have their ups and downs, and that what is striking about South Africa's is its resilience over a long period. Advocates of this approach stress that in the post-war years only the Japanese economy has had a higher overall growth rate. For instance, through all the uncertainties of the 1960s the South African economy had a growth rate of almost 6 per cent per annum, and despite the rapid rise in the population the per capita income rose by almost 3 per cent in the same period.[5] They also argue that the crises which have overtaken South Africa have been financial rather than structural, and that the ingredients of future strength have been laid – with great mineral wealth allied to a strong manufacturing base, a plentiful supply of labour, a successful agricultural industry, and a well-developed infrastructure. They argue that South Africa has demonstrated both steady growth over a long period and the ability to respond to change.

These different interpretations point to quite distinctive strategies for British businessmen and investors. If it is largely a windfall economy, the wise course is to take quick advantage of what exists, and then run. In contrast, if the long-term growth economy is the right analysis, there is every reason to become heavily embroiled and well established. Of course the decisions are seldom perceived in such crude terms. Usually there is a mixture of assumptions, and for many British companies in South Africa there is not much flexibility, even if confidence is low, for a substantial part of the British stake is in the form of local subsidiaries of British parent companies, in holdings in South African enterprises and in investment which cannot easily be realized. With such limited options the best strategy may be to sit tight and hope for better days, but the uncertainties may well have decided new companies against moving into the Republic, or those already there against continuing to develop.

In 1970 Wates, the British building company, announced that it would not enter the South African market because of political uncertainties and opposition to the racial policies of the government.[6] In October 1980 Mr A. C. Briggs, the South African chairman of the South Africa–Britain Trade Association (SABRITA), estimated that British companies under political pressure had disinvested by £250m from South Africa over the previous three and a half years, although he quickly pointed out that this was from a total of about £5,000m.[7] A different and perhaps more typical British business response was given by Lord Erroll of Hale, the chairman of Consolidated Gold Fields, who told the shareholders: 'Gold Fields is confident in the long-term prosperity of South Africa, but it has to be recognized that there may be periods of internal unrest from time to time. During such periods many investors take a gloomy view of South Africa's long-term future. Gold Fields may be a net buyer of South African assets at such times.'[8] In other words, Gold Fields were determined to take advantage of the downs as well as the ups.

One reason for the contradictory judgements of the South African economy is the role played by gold. Gold has always been treated as something apart, almost mystical in its qualities and therefore unlike other goods that are traded or exchanged. Like the attractions of a beautiful woman, it is to be appreciated but not treated with confidence. Thus, although it plays a major part in the South African economy, its sale is not usually included in the balance-of-trade figures, which consequently show an unhealthy deficit that is usually more than covered by the gold sales. The uncertainty surrounding gold extends to its place in the international monetary system, and South Africa, by far the largest supplier outside the communist bloc, is deeply caught up in the 'political' controversies about its price and supply.

The USA has played a prominent part in these conflicts. Throughout the 1960s and 1970s, in what were known as the 'gold battles', it led assaults that were intended to bring down the price and/or to break gold's link with the monetary system. In this, it was opposed by states with large gold holdings, like France, Switzerland and Italy, as well as by South Africa.

The USA was partly influenced by political objectives in these gold battles. According to R. W. Johnson, one of its purposes during another conflict over gold – in 1974–5 – was to force the South Africans into accepting American initiatives in Africa. Other reasons for wanting to depress the price of gold were 'putting the French in their place, reducing the value of Russian gold sales, and asserting the primacy of the dollar.'[9] For a time US policy succeeded and gold prices fell from $200 in January 1975 to $130 in January 1976. However, again the position could not be held. As world recession developed in the late 1970s, as inflation persisted and as fears of East/West confrontation were revived, so there was a flight back into gold. Gold prices leapt ahead – reaching $850 per ounce in January 1980 – benefiting the South African balance of payments and also demonstrating the declining ability of the Americans to control the international economy. Since then the price has fallen, but has settled down to a level much higher than that of the mid-1970s. At the beginning of 1982 it was just over $400.

Gold, therefore, has introduced one area of uncertainty: another is related to decision-taking about economic links. Pressures to reduce economic ties with South Africa, whether they come at international gatherings or from anti-apartheid groups at home, are often directed at the British government in the belief that the government can and should play a leading role in reducing or even eliminating the ties. In practice most decisions are made by private companies. Even if the British government wanted to change that, and there is little evidence that it does, there must be doubts about its ability to supervise and control the multiplicity of the decisions required. Furthermore, the structure of many business organizations operates against tight government control – partly because so many multinationals are involved in South Africa, and partly because many of the British firms operating in the Republic rely on local managerial staff.

The British government's main role in these relations has been to create a climate for economic activity – by easing or intensifying political pressures, by being more or less helpful in export guarantees, by organizing trade fairs, by encouraging or discouraging overseas investment, and by forming advisory bodies of government officials and business interests. With a few exceptions, its approach has been to try to treat economic links as separate from other relations and to encourage them, and this has been especially marked in the departments responsible for the economy, including the Bank of England. However, it has never been able to persuade the opponents of apartheid that it is possible to separate the economy in this way.

Exceptions to Britain's general approach have been the ban on arms sales in 1977 (when the UN mandatory embargo was adopted) – which of course has economic implications – and the increasing concern shown in the Labour government of the late 1970s about the degree of Britain's economic reliance on South Africa. That concern prompted the government to start investigating the implications of disinvestment and disengagement to reduce the country's vulnerability, but Labour did not remain in power long enough to decide whether or not to translate concern into practice. If it had gone ahead, the scale of the impact is uncertain, for – short of imposing mandatory sanctions – the government's ability to control international economic transactions is declining, as relationships grow more complex, and as more and more business and financial institutions are organized along multinational lines. The increased size and spread of interests among companies make them less dependent on any one area or market. Therefore it could be argued that they can more easily accept a break with South Africa, but those very characteristics of size and diversity also make them less vulnerable to governments or international organizations which, for political reasons, want to increase the pressures on South Africa.

Having examined various factors which have to be taken into account in assessing Britain's economic stake, we can now turn to the broad areas of activity in the bilateral relationship. These are identified under the following headings: trade, investment, banking and minerals.

Trade
South Africa and Britain are traditionally major trading partners. Since Britain has the larger economy, the flow of trade between the two countries naturally represents a smaller proportion of its total trade. Thus, in 1976, while Britain's £632m of exports to South Africa, and £714m of imports, represented 2.5 per cent and 2.3 per cent, respectively, of total export and import trade, the South African proportions were 22.2 per cent of exports (excluding gold) and 17.6 per cent of imports. In terms of value, the bilateral trade has risen steadily over the post-war years, but it has fallen as a proportion of the total international trade of both countries. This was particularly noticeable during the 1970s. Earlier the South African slice of Britain's total world trade had remained remarkably stable, usually lying between 3 and 4 per cent. There was a set-back following the political upheavals in the early 1960s, but that was followed by a trade boom in the mid-1960s, when the 4 per cent figure was breached twice; from 1968, however, the relative size of the trade began to diminish. By 1971 it was down to 4.4 per cent and continued to fall (with the exception of a brief rally in 1975) until 1980, when it represented only 2.1 per cent of the British total. The 1970s also saw a change in the balance of trade

between the two countries. While for most of the post-war years Britain enjoyed a favourable balance with South Africa, the situation then became more evenly poised, and in 1978 the balance was against Britain. It exported £667m to the Republic but imported £911m of goods. By 1980, however, British exports were ahead again, with £1,002m against imports of £756m, and remained that way in 1981.

Until the last few years Britain was the main single market for South African goods: in 1967, for example, South Africa sent roughly one-third of its goods to Britain. By the early 1980s, however, Britain was taking less than 10 per cent of South Africa's exports, and was grouped with the USA, West Germany and Japan. It had lost its pre-eminence but remained an important market. As for Britain's principal imports from South Africa, these can be grouped into three main areas: (*a*) food, in which fruit, vegetables, and animal and fish products play significant parts; (*b*) 'crude inedible materials', a classification that includes hides, pulp, waste paper, textiles and scrap metals; and (*c*) minerals, which together form the most valuable group of imports, but they are not classified together in the trade figures, for gold has always been treated separately, and diamonds are placed under the misleading heading of 'manufacturing goods'.

Similarly, for most of the post-war years Britain was the chief supplier of goods to South Africa, but – again during the 1970s – it lost its pre-eminence while remaining an important exporter. As with imports, it now shares a leading position with the USA, West Germany and Japan. Also South Africa's place in the British export league has fallen as British trade has become more Europe-orientated. In 1967 South Africa was third, and by 1977 it had fallen sharply to sixteenth, although by 1980 it had made a slight recovery to twelfth. As with imports, broad patterns can be identified in British exports to South Africa, although here there is greater diversity. Between 1974 and 1977, three main categories of British exports – electrical equipment, transport equipment and other machinery – constituted between 52 per cent and 60 per cent of the total exports to South Africa. During these years, however, the balance among them changed, with a decline in transport equipment following the imposition of the arms embargo and the virtual disappearance of British cars after the closure of the British Leyland plant. In contrast, chemicals showed a steady increase, moving from 6.6 per cent of British exports in 1967 to 13.4 per cent in 1977. Nevertheless there was no one sector of British exports which South Africa dominated, and by the late 1970s in no single trade category did it take more than 5 per cent of the total. However, although the figures indicate the sectors of British industry which directly export to South Africa, they do not reveal the full spread of involvement. Since most British exports to the Republic are in sophisticated manufacturing goods, many sectors of British industry are involved in the production process. Thus, while 'electrical equipment' as a category indicates the nature of the finished article, the economic activity is spread widely and is certainly not confined to electrical firms.

An area of activity in which British firms are involved but which does not appear in the terms of trade is the supply of oil and its products. The British companies BP and Shell supply about a third of South Africa's needs of about 400,000 barrels each day from their refinery at Durban, which is the largest in the Republic. Until 1978 the bulk of South Africa's oil came from Iran, but following the revolution that source of supply was lost, and so South Africa had to purchase in the spot market, paying a high premium in times of scarcity. However, although the source of the oil changed, the role of the British multinational companies did not. They continued to help supply South Africa's oil needs.

Investment

Three initial points can be made about British investment in South Africa: it is large; it is profitable; and much of the profit is reinvested in the Republic. As with trade, Britain is traditionally the main outside partner and it has retained this position in terms of total investment, although the position of London as South Africa's main financial centre is not so clear-cut. As the SABRITA chairman, A. C. Briggs, pointed out in 1980: 'The London Stock Exchange used to be the world centre for South African securities, and to a certain extent this is still so today, although Zürich is also important to the Johannesburg Stock Exchange.'[10] He re-emphasized, however, that Britain remained by far the largest investor, as the figures confirm. Although during the 1960s, and even more noticeably during the 1970s, US, West German and French investment increased, Britain has remained the largest single investor, accounting for about 37 per cent of all South Africa's foreign liabilities in 1976.

Although the broad picture of British investment in South Africa can be drawn, the fine detail must always be open to some doubt, because of uncertainties about the different forms that investment takes, because of the difficulty of making valuations on assumed market prices, and because of the secrecy which surrounds South African investment. Yet what can confidently be said is that the Republic has proved a very profitable field for British investments. It is estimated that roughly 10 per cent of all British overseas investments are in South Africa, but the rate of return has often been about 16 per cent of the total, and despite occasional crises and predictions of impending internal collapse, the high profits have usually ensured a continuous supply of foreign capital. As an international banker is reported to have said in 1980: 'If it were not for the political stigma, South Africa would be the bluest of blue chips. As it is, the rate of return and its reliability now clearly outweigh the political problems.'[11]

British investment in South Africa is divided between 'direct' investment (i.e., when a firm invests or reinvests in its own activities or that of a subsidiary in South Africa) and 'indirect' investment (i.e., the purchase of shares in a South African company and loans to companies or the government). According to one study, it is indirect investment that has been growing more quickly: thus, by the end of 1976, whereas direct British investment (excluding oil, banking and insurance) was worth £1,263m, the indirect (plus that in oil, banking and insurance) was as high as £3,554m.[12] A further characteristic is that British investment is spread widely across the South African economy: in paper and printing, in mining and quarrying, in the distributive trades, and so on. This spread includes not only private industry, but public enterprises which have grown as the South African government has become increasingly involved in the economy. This was demonstrated in 1980 with the floating of a Eurobond for DM120m, and a syndicated credit of $250m, which were arranged through a number of banks, some in Switzerland and West Germany, but also British banks, including Standard and Barclays.

Banking

Although most British banks are involved in South Africa in one way or another, the two giants are Barclays and Standard, which operate directly through South African subsidiaries. In 1977 the percentage share of the total commercial bank deposits were estimated to be: Barclays 35.6 per cent, Standard 26.6 per cent, Volkas 18.0 per cent, Trust (Bankorp) 10.4 per cent and Nedbank 9.4 per cent.[13] While the Afrikaner banks have developed their business around the agricultural community, Afrikaner business, the government and local authorities, Barclays and Standard have concentrated more on the private sectors of industry and mining, especially those with British connections – including Anglo-American, Gold Fields of South Africa, AECI and BP.

However, the banks emphasize that their activities are not confined to big business or whites. In 1971 Sir Frederic Seebohm, the chairman of Barclays, said that the bank had 700,000 non-white customers, and added that it had done its best 'to give good service to *all races*'.[14] Over recent years Standard and Barclays have extended their business from that of commercial banks to cover hire-purchase, leasing, credit cards, management services, insurance banking, unit trusts and merchant banking. In the merchant banking field they, together with Hill Samuel (a British merchant bank), are among the top five in South Africa. In addition, British banks (and this has certainly not been confined to Standard and Barclays) have been well placed to keep open South Africa's channels with the international financial markets. While South Africa is able to generate considerable domestic capital, it has also drawn on foreign capital to finance major new developments both in the private and in the public fields. British banks have played a significant part in servicing these loans and in placing their own investments in South Africa. Reliable figures are difficult to find, but a CCSA report estimated that in the period 1972-6, as South Africa undertook a large programme of 'strategic investment', its total indebtedness to international banks rose from \$3.3bn to \$8.6bn, and that British banks were responsible for raising almost half of the increase.[15] This is not surprising, since London, with its banking expertise, is a major centre for raising capital, including Eurobonds and Eurocurrency loans which the South Africans have favoured. In the single year 1975-6, Hill Samuel (South Africa) claimed to have negotiated international loans for the equivalent of \$520m for the Republic.

Minerals

South Africa has great wealth in minerals. These can be divided into three main categories, based on their use: (*a*) fuel and energy, such as uranium and coal; (*b*) industrial and high technology, such as chrome and platinum; and (*c*) precious metals, including gold and diamonds. Western states make extensive use of all three categories, and South Africa's importance is further increased by the focal part it plays in the mineral industries of neighbouring black states. It provides transport and communication, skilled manpower, technology and capital for these industries. Trade in minerals is usually recorded in terms of a movement between countries, with, in this case, a mutual reliance between South Africa as a source and the Western states as the market. An alternative approach is to concentrate on the activities of the major multinational companies, for the world of minerals, with its high technology, great risks, complex transport arrangements and huge investments, is dominated by large companies. In exceptional cases a single company may come to dominate a sector of the industry, as De Beers has with diamonds. 'When "Namibia" is described as having exported 1.69 million carats of diamonds in 1977, the reality is that one subsidiary of De Beers Consolidated (in this case Consolidated Diamond Mines) is transferring the diamonds it has mined to another De Beers subsidiary in London.'[16]

More usually, however, there are many interests involved, and whether the emphasis is on country, government or company, a complex picture emerges of interdependent diverse interests. The minerals may be mined in one country by a company with its home base in another, processed in a third, and then used in industrial processes in a fourth. Uranium from Namibia provides such an example. The uranium concentrate is mined in a territory which is controlled by South Africa, but is subject to international dispute. The uranium mine itself, at Rossing, is operated by a British multinational company, Rio Tinto Zinc (RTZ), which exports the mineral to countries like France, Britain and the USA for a conversion process that is carried out mainly by government-controlled agencies, but in the case of the USA by private companies. This is followed by an enriching process which is under government control, and then the fuel elements are distributed to reactors around the world. With such interdependence it would be an over-simplification to suggest that any single company, government or authority has a dominant position.

There are a number of ways in which Britain is involved in the South African mineral industry. These are, first, the part played by British mining companies in the extraction, processing, transport and trading of the minerals; second, British investment in the industry; third, the London mineral markets; and, fourth, the import of South African minerals into Britain. A number of major British mining companies operate in the Republic – notably Consolidated Gold Fields, Selection Trust (now owned by BP), Lonrho and RTZ. Although these are large companies, their combined operation probably constitutes no more than 5 per cent of the total South African mining industry. This estimate is based on direct British investment in the industry, which in 1975 had a book value of £91m in a total for the Republic of about £2,000m.[17] Nevertheless, the South African industry is so large that even 5 per cent of it represents an important part of the activities of these firms.

The scale of the South African mining operation in relation to their other interests varies considerably between the companies. For Consolidated Gold Fields, South Africa represents the major part of its activities, whereas Lonrho has a spread of interests throughout Africa and elsewhere, of which mining is only one, and similarly RTZ has widely spread global mining interests. However, to illustrate the British interest, RTZ can be taken as an example. The company grew rapidly during the 1960s and 1970s and, although its operations are world-wide, with mines in Australia, Canada and New Zealand as well as southern Africa, its activities in the subcontinent have been especially successful. It has three major mines there: the Palabora copper mine in South Africa itself, which produces roughly half the Republic's total copper production of about 220,000 tons per year; the Empress nickel mine in Zimbabwe, which during the perid of UDI was managed separately by a breakaway RTZ subsidiary; and the Rossing open-cast uranium mine in Namibia, which is a major world producer. The Rossing operation is the basis of a contract first approved by Mr Tony Benn for the Labour government for the supply of uranium from Namibia to the British Central Electricity Generating Board. The success of these southern African operations helps to explain the company's ability in September 1980 to launch the biggest rights issue seen in the City for many years – raising £126m.

When we turn to the second aspect of British involvement – investment in the mining industry – the information available is dated and not always reliable. Nevertheless the operation of large companies like RTZ itself represents a considerable stake. Investment in mining probably accounts for about 10 per cent of total *direct* British investment (excluding oil, banking and insurance). The figures at the beginning of 1975 were £91m assets in mining from a total direct British investment of £997m, with the exceptions noted above.[18] There is also considerable indirect investment. Britain has traditionally exported capital, as part of the 'invisible earnings' that help its balance of payments, and the South African mines have been part of this area of activity, with their large demand for capital and the prospect of good profits. That position continues, and has, indeed, improved as a result of the removal of exchange controls by the Thatcher government.

Britain is also involved in the marketing of South African minerals. Founded on confidence that has been built up over the years and traditional financial and marketing skills, London is a major market for many of the world's minerals – including gold and diamonds – and the London metal market sets prices that are universally recognized. This does not imply that the minerals need pass through Britain, but rather that the trading, price-fixing and broking are done there. These markets provide for minerals some services that are similar to those of the City in financial transactions. South Africa's minerals are, of course, only part of the trade, but in some sectors they can be of considerable importance. For example, South Africans' decisions about where to send their gold and their diamonds greatly affects the size and activity of the main markets.

The final British involvement is in the purchase of minerals for its own use. The following figures for British imports of selected minerals show the importance of the trade: in 1977–8, South Africa supplied 70 per cent of Britain's chrome ore, 54 per cent of its manganese ore, 65 per cent of its platinum group metals, and 66 per cent of its gold. It is on the import side that those who emphasize Britain's stake in the South African mineral industry lay the greatest stress. It would doubtless harm the British economy if the large British mining companies could no longer operate in South Africa, or the London metal markets no longer handled South African goods, or British investment in the industry gave little or no reward, but the threat to the supply of minerals is said to be of a different order. It is, according to this view, not simply a matter of the quantity of minerals that Britain imports from the Republic, but that some of these minerals are 'vital', and, without the South African supply, sections of British industry would be crippled. If that is the case, then plainly Britain has a large stake in the South African mineral industry. But some people, both in South Africa and in Britain, overstate the case. In the first place, the picture can change quite rapidly, as it has with uranium, for which the demand has been less than anticipated and for which new sources of supply have been found. Furthermore, there are alternative sources or substitutes for other South African minerals, such as copper, nickel, iron, phosphate, zinc, silver and lead.

However, there are a few South African minerals for which at present there are no easy substitutes or alternative sources of supply for Britain. These are the platinum group, chrome and manganese (and perhaps gold should be included).[19] With the experience of the oil crisis in mind, this is a position of vulnerability which few in Britain relish, irrespective of their political commitment. During his period of office, David Owen persistently warned against it and urged less reliance on the Republic.

Not everybody would accept such a bleak picture. An alternative argument is advanced that, although there would be difficulties, market forces would quickly start to rectify the position by discovering alternative sources, finding substitute materials, recycling existing stocks, developing new technologies and end-products. A further point which is made is that the trade in minerals is so important to the South African economy that whoever has political control, or whatever the situation inside the country, the minerals will continue to find their way out. Moreover, even if there were some interruptions in the flow it would not have anything like the impact of changes in the world's oil supply, for that affects virtually every aspect of the Western economies, whereas the absence or slowing down of South African mineral supplies would be restricted to certain sectors of the economy, and the effects could be contained.

As far as Britain is concerned, there is an element of risk, whatever side of the argument is taken. Britain's vulnerability depends on a number of interrelated factors: the use to which the minerals are put, the degree of dependence on South Africa, the opportunity to switch to alternative sources, the availability of substitute materials, and the time required to readjust to sudden changes. On all these counts, Britain is potentially vulnerable in some minerals, and is more exposed than some other Western states. France, for one, has a wider spread of sources, with its chrome, for instance, coming from Malagasy, Turkey and the USSR. Similarly, in 1977 South Africa provided only 12 per cent of France's imports of the platinum group as against 65 per cent of Britain's. Nevertheless, the British response (whether it be the government, the mining companies or the industrial users) may be to do very little – whether out of complacency, from failure to agree, because of the enormous costs involved, or because the risk is thought to be tolerable.

In balancing such risks, the considerable attractions of the existing situation in South Africa for foreign mining companies comes into play. South Africa is a low-cost producer (partly because of easy access to minerals, and partly through cheap labour), it has liberal tax laws which encourage reinvestment, and its domestic energy supplies are cheap.

Unlike some other mineral producers, it has a good reputation in fulfilling its commercial contracts, it has not introduced restrictive ownership policies or nationalization, and the profits have been excellent. Added to all this, the alternative sources of supply for some minerals are in areas that are potentially even more unstable or are in the communist bloc. Several of the world's known resources of minerals are virtually shared between South Africa and the USSR, as the following table shows (1978 percentage of world total):

	South Africa	USSR	Total
Reserves			
Chromium.....................................	68	<1	69
Manganese....................................	37	50	87
Vanadium.....................................	19	74	93
Platinum-group metals	73	25	98
Gold...	48	22	70
Production			
Chromium.....................................	34	32	66
Manganese....................................	23	43	66
Vanadium.....................................	39	31	70
Platinum-group metals..................	46	47	93
Gold...	58	20	78

Source: US Bureau of Mines, *Mineral Commodity Summaries, 1979* (Washington, D.C., 1979).

For all its problems, therefore, the South Africa mineral balance-sheet has continued to look healthier than the alternatives. However, the dangers are clear. There are four main reasons why supplies of minerals from South Africa might be cut off or substantially reduced: first, retaliation by the present white government – for example, as a reaction against limited economic sanctions; second, a decision by the Western governments to impose mandatory economic sanctions, even if taken reluctantly and under great pressure; third, the establishment of a black pro-communist government which might ally with the USSR in trying to cut the West's jugular by dominating the Cape route and denying vital minerals (although this view is strongly challenged); fourth, and perhaps the most likely possibility, major internal disorder and urban conflict leading to severe disruption in supply.

There are a number of strategies open to Britain and other Western states to try to lessen the dangers, but none is easy, cheap or quick. One option is to find alternative suppliers, but, as noted, this is not always possible and, when the main alternative is the USSR, carries a potential security risk. Another is to explore for new sources or develop those which are known but have not so far been exploited – the stock of exploitable minerals being flexible according to price, technology and successful exploration. However, this is slow and very expensive – as usually is the third possibility, which is to develop substitutes. Finally, there is the option of stockpiling.

Some Western states, such as the USA and France (but not Britain), have done this, but there are problems here too. One is that if many Western states were to stockpile, there might be panic-buying, wild market fluctuations and shortages, so that some of the potential problems which stockpiling was designed to overcome would be self-induced. Another uncertainty concerns the nature of the stockpile, for it is impossible to cover all dangers. US policy is to stockpile materials required for direct military use, but European thinking has been more on wider industrial needs. Then there is the problem of stockpiles going out of date – of yesterday's 'vital' minerals no longer being required – leaving the task of disposing of the unwanted supplies. Moreover, even if stockpiles are built up, they can only be shock absorbers, giving short-term relief while an alternative source or a substitute material is found, or while the problems which have affected supplies are ironed out. Finally, in all the schemes there is the question of who pays. Should the huge costs involved be shouldered by the government, by the mining companies, by industrial users, or by a combination of all three? No one is eager to take on the burden, and each employs its considerable powers to try to move the responsibility elsewhere.

Evaluating the economic stake
Clearly, Britain's economic stake cannot be accurately quantified, not just because of the limitations of the statistics themselves, but because of the difficulty of making objective judgements – both about the relative importance of different aspects of the economic relationship, and about the emphasis that is placed on economic aims in relation to others. Even apparently straightforward questions like 'Who benefits from the economic relationship?' and 'Do the British government and British business have the same interests?' are open to very different interpretations. On the question of who benefits, there are different views about whether it is South Africa or Britain, and also, from another approach, whether, as the business community argues, the relationship is beneficial to all the people of Britain and South Africa, or, as some critics argue, only to the dominant capitalist class. As to the second question, the picture is complicated, with the government sharing some interests with the business community, but, because it has a variety of aims and is subject to a variety of pressures, the interests it pursues and the methods it employs do not always coincide with those of the business community.

This point is brought home in comments made by Sir Arthur Snelling on Rhodesian sanctions. Sir Arthur, who had been a senior official at the Commonwealth Office, and had been responsible for advising on and implementing the sanctions policy under the Wilson government, said that he had made a number of proposals for ways of tightening the sanctions, but 'it soon became clear that any such intensification was not on because if would have been extremely unpopular in the City of London and with the Conservative Party, and the net result would have been a state of economic warfare not just between Britain and Rhodesia but between Whitehall and the City of London, and that was not on for bipartisan reasons.'[20]

Another way of trying to evaluate Britain's overall economic stake is to try to estimate the effect of cutting off all economic links between the two countries. While that may seem an improbable situation, estimates of the possible consequences have been made in the frequent debates about the possibility of mandatory UN sanctions against the Republic. Considerable efforts have been put into these evaluations, but, as ever, there is no agreement. Uncertainties and conflicting assumptions abound. Would firms be able to find alternative markets or sources of supply? How effective would the sanctions prove to be? Would South Africa be able to retaliate and, if so, in what way? Would Britain's trading rivals take advantage of the situation? How would the black states respond if Britain failed to act against the Republic? Would the critical minerals prove to be 'critical'? What effect would there be on employment in Britain?

The answers that are given are deeply coloured by the political commitments of their authors. Two reports published in 1979 make this point very clear: the one, *Britain's Economic Links with South Africa*, is written by two strong oponents of South Africa, Bernard Rivers and Martin Bailey; the other, *British Trade with South Africa*, emanates from the business pressure group UKSATA.[21] In calculating the effect on employment in Britain of cutting links with South Africa, Rivers and Bailey, basing their calculations on the assumption that British firms would almost immediately be able to replace at least half their South African markets, conclude that the maximum figure made unemployed would be 20,000 in any one year, and that it would start to trail off after three years. The UKSATA pamphlet takes a much more dramatic view: a direct loss of 70,000 jobs, followed later by a multiplier effect within the economy, plus the loss of vital mineral supplies, which 'would probably result in a huge rise in unemployment, perhaps as much as 180,000 above the estimated 70,000'.[22] The UKSATA total therefore reaches a possible 250,000 compared with the 20,000 of Rivers and Bailey. No further comment is needed.

4 The Search for Values

As the discussion of the economic stake makes clear, the relationship with South Africa presents the British with a dilemma over values. This has been sharpened by the increased international awareness of racial issues, and in Britain by the development of a multiracial society. In the past, the South African relationship was complicated by efforts to build a multiracial Commonwealth – an endeavour which stirred an emotional commitment in Britain which has not been matched in other relationships, including those with the countries of the European Community. Although many of Britain's hopes for the Commonwealth were dashed, the values which were invoked in the effort – covering relations between rich and poor nations, and peoples of different races and creeds – are ones that raise strong British reactions.

With this general debate, what explains the degree of attention and bitterness that South Africa generates in Britain and in the international community? South Africa is set apart on four counts. First, it is unique in the way that it uses formal legislation, based on race, to preserve and create divisions among its people. The discriminatory legislative framework of the society is comprehensive – covering such matters as where people may live, what schools they may attend and what trains they may take – and is applied with great determination by a large bureaucracy and a ruthless police force.

Second, discrimination by race has been perceived in the international community as an offence against a 'cosmopolitan justice':[1] i.e., a concern which involves mankind as a whole. The concern for racial cosmopolitan justice is extended further by some radicals, who see South Africa as part of the struggle of the world's oppressed against capitalist exploitation. Thus, in South Africa's case, race and class become merged in a wider commitment to a new order and a new justice. This radical dimension, when married to a concern for individual rights, explains why most states are agreed on the 'injustice' of apartheid. Whereas Western states tend to emphasize the individual, the black states and communist governments lay greater emphasis on structural injustice, on the way society is organized to deny rights to a race and/or a class. In South Africa's case the offence is both to the individual and to the blacks collectively – so West,

East and black states combine in condemning it.

Third, the black states are prepared to override the respect for state rights which they usually underline in defending their own sovereignty, because they see the Republic as the last act in the drama of decolonization which has transformed Asia and Africa from a world of empires to one of sovereign, independent states. It may be possible also to see Western hostility to South Africa in this context – as a sense of guilt for the colonial past. Explaining its decision to support the World Council of Churches' programme to combat racism, the British Methodist Conference in 1979 spoke of an era of 400 years of white domination in which the church had shared, and concluded that 'the church has to identify itself particularly with those who have suffered as a result of the evil of racism'. Other Britons may be less concerned with guilt, but in rationalizing the end of imperial control they have come to accept racial equality as a norm, even if not one that is universally observed.

Finally, in explaining why the criticism against South Africa is so strong and so widespread, a fourth factor has to be introduced – what has been called 'the vagaries of international politics'.[2] In other states in which basic individual and group rights are regularly infringed, the political settings have been different. Thus, for example, although atrocities are reported from Ethiopia, there are no United Nations members or pressure groups inside the Western states which are committed against the Ethiopian government, nor has the situation there been seen as an infringement of universal rights – as racialism and capitalist exploitation have been perceived in South Africa. Equally, although the Western states have persistently criticized breaches of human rights in the USSR, in that case the political forces are so finely balanced, and the dangers to international peace so great, that the point is not pressed to a conclusion; international order is given priority over individual justice. In South Africa's case, however, the strength of the moral indignation is matched by the strength of the political forces ranged against the country.

Three bands of opinion

In Britain, although there is no agreed position on South Africa, or even the elements of a consensus, attitudes to race relations have moved steadily against the racial discrimination on which white supremacy in the Republic is based. Some segments of the community might choose to ignore apartheid, but few would support it. Broadly speaking, three bands of opinion can be identified: 'conservative', 'liberal' and 'radical'. The conservative view, which emphasizes state rights, is that potential conflict exists between justice and order, but it gives its priority to order, believing that the fragile balance on which order is built can very easily be destroyed. The radical view also sees an inherent conflict, but in this case takes justice as the commanding value and is prepared to accept a break-down of order. The breakdown is not permanent, however, for a new order will be created which offers the justice that is sought. The liberal approach is reluctant to accept the conflict, for it believes that order is maintained by righting injustices; that the breakdown of order may result in even greater injustice; and that, however difficult it may be, consensus can be achieved.

The three bands of opinion are exemplified in the attitudes of prominent individuals. Sir Alec Douglas-Home, during his period as foreign secretary, was an advocate of the conservative approach, as was made clear in his address to the 1970 Conservative Party Conference.[3] At that time controversy was raging in both Britain and the Commonwealth about the announcement that the new Conservative administration was considering selling arms to South Africa. In commenting on this, Sir Alec did not concentrate narrowly on South Africa, but pointed out, rather, that Britain's aims were to establish a peaceful world in which trade and commerce could prosper. Britain must therefore play its part in creating international stability and collective security. This could in part be achieved by pursuing its economic and strategic interests in Europe, but also there was the need to combine in broader terms against the Soviet threat. He explained his fears of the growing strength of the Soviet fleet, which threatened to dominate the Mediterranean Sea and the Indian Ocean, and it was in this context that he set South Africa. On the arms sale issue, he said that the British government was pleased to listen to the viewpoint of the Commonwealth members, but they, on their side, must listen rationally to the views of Britain.

Sir Alec then moved to another area of concern which had direct relevance to South Africa – attitudes towards the guerrilla fighters of exiled nationalist movements. He said that they were outside the law, and that he opposed any support for them. Not only did their activities threaten the present international order, but they undermined the principle of non-interference in the affairs of sovereign states.

There are other sides to the conservative approach in Britain. One dimension was developed by Edward Norman, the Dean of Peterhouse College, Cambridge, in the BBC Reith lectures of 1978. Norman, who entitled his lectures 'Christianity and World Order', concentrated on what he called 'the politicization of Christianity'.[4] He saw this as a process whereby a set of political and social values had become the central tenets of reinterpreted Christianity. These ideas were advanced with all the confidence of those who had found eternal truth, whereas for Norman they were necessarily relative and unstable, reflecting the shifting social values of the day. Norman, who stated that he personally opposed apartheid, recognized that South Africa was a major concern for this new Christianity because the values which it embraced were built on opposition to what were seen as collective sins, such as racism and economic exploitation. These views, said Norman, were advanced not by the oppressed of the earth but by a Westernized elite who claimed to speak for the oppressed. Naive liberal Christian leaders followed meekly behind – led on by their concern with social issues and human rights but in fact supporting doctrines of radical social change, often founded on anti-religious Marxist beliefs, and usually implying a revolutionary process which would bring suffering and hardship for the very people it was supposed to help. Another feature, according to Norman, was the double standard of their judgement. Infringements of human rights in South Africa or Chile were castigated, whereas those in Tanzania or the East European communist states were ignored; accusations of racism were confined to white racism, while other forms were glossed over.

One of the most persistent advocates of the liberal approach has been David Owen, foreign secretary in the Labour government between 1977 and 1979, who is deeply committed to southern African affairs. In an address in London to mark Anti-Apartheid Year, he described apartheid as 'institutionalized racism'. It was also a form of political suicide, he said. Since it could not survive, the only questions were when and how it would be ended. Recent developments in Mozambique and Angola had demonstrated that change could be achieved through violence, and it could happen in South Africa: it was incumbent on those who believed in liberal and democratic values to work for change through peaceful means. Moreover, speed was important, for, 'Delay allows communist ideology to flourish and in the final trauma of change chaos emerges as the real threat.'[5]

In contrast to Home, who saw communism as the great external threat, Owen's concern was with the internal policies of the South African government. In his attitude to apartheid, he described himself as 'a radical reformer, not a gradualist', but he admitted that the liberal view was not easy to communicate. It did not have the simple (oversimple, he believed) message of the far right or the far left. The liberal message assumes that reasoned change can be achieved; it eschews violence and welcomes diversity of opinion.

Although Owen emphasized the moral issues, he also recognized that hard-headed business interests were involved, and that what had been built up over generations could not be altered overnight. While care should be taken not to drive the white South Africans to desperation, especially with the threat that they might develop nuclear weapons, sustained pressure must be applied. With that in mind, he defended strongly the government's support for the EEC Code of Conduct for firms operating in South Africa. What was needed, he said, was to restore confidence in the process of discussion and negotiation.

The views and aims which Owen developed in his speeches are also found in his book *Human Rights*. In this, he states that he cannot condemn as enemies of democracy those who, like the nationalist movements in the Portuguese territories, have fought for their rights. Furthermore, to interpret the conflict in Africa as a straight clash between East and West is to play into the hands of the USSR by convincing Africans that the West has no moral commitments and in fact supports apartheid. 'Our task', he writes, '. . . is to demonstrate change can be brought about rapidly and effectively by peaceful means'.[6]

For an example of the radical approach, we do not have to turn to the exiled black nationalists or even to the Anti-Apartheid Movement. It is to be found in a report issued by the British Council of Churches in 1970. The report was the work of a mixed committee of laymen and clergy, chaired by Philip Mason, then director of the Institute of Race Relations. As its title implies – *Violence in Southern Africa: A Christian Assessment* – the report concentrated on the Christian's dilemma in judging the use of violence to achieve change.[7] It came down squarely for those who believed that violence was justified when used against gross injustice. In the section entitled 'Revolution, the Church and the Kingdom', the group noted that the injustices and cruelties of government had often been ignored because the first priority had been given to stability. In consequence, a 'negative' view had been taken of revolution. That needed rethinking. The churches should consider adopting a 'theology of revolution', in which the principal aims were the struggle for justice on earth and the teaching of Christ.

The committee recognized that in many societies this would imply radical change, and 'in southern Africa the radical change is not to be hoped for without revolution'. Admittedly, there were individuals, like Gandhi, Luthuli and Martin Luther King, who rejected violence, even to the point of martyrdom, but they were exceptional. Most people accepted forms of violence, and it was hypocritical of the British to urge non-violence in southern Africa while accepting that there could be just war to defend their own country.

While not denying that the path of violence seldom leads directly to justice, the members of the group were insistent that the church should declare its 'solidarity with the *aims* of the revolution in southern Africa'. They held out no hope for gradual reform, believing that violent revolution was the only redress open for the oppressed, but if the church were directly involved it could help to 'humanize' revolution.

Another version of the radical approach came in the series of Reith lectures which followed Edward Norman's – indicating again the prominent position South Africa enjoys in moral and political debate in

Britain. The 1979 lectures – 'The African Condition' – were given by Professor Ali Mazrui.[8] Since Mazrui is not British, it may be argued that his views should not be seen as part of the British debate, but the strength of the reactions which he produced (hostile as well as sympathetic) demonstrates their relevance.

In examining the position of the South African whites, Mazrui had none of the liberals' hopes that reason and compromise would achieve reform, nor did he share the conservatives' fears of disorder. He was clear that it was only through revolutionary struggle that 'the amalgam of slavery and colonization' which existed in South Africa could be overthrown. He pointed out that there was no precedent for any white settler community in Africa giving up its power without violence, and South Africa would be no exception. Revolution would have to be waged from within the country. There would be some external backing, but because it would largely be an internal struggle he did not take seriously the threat of nuclear war in southern Africa.

The Western powers were clearly associated with apartheid, but unwittingly they would help forward the revolution because they would continue to exert pressure for reform on the South Africans. There was no chance that this would achieve reform by itself, but it would open up opportunities for the revolutionaries, as would economic expansion leading to the growth of a proletariat. 'My own conviction', Mazrui said, 'is that conditions of violent revolution in a racially segregated society can best be created in conditions where new economic classes drawn from the oppressed are demanding new rewards, and there is sufficient freedom in the society to enable revolutionaries to recruit and organize for the final confrontation with the system of injustice.'[9] Unlike many other radicals, he believed that the West would be wise to continue its economic contacts, but should at the same time give support to the liberation movements, not necessarily in the supply of arms, but in the form of funds and moral backing. He also commented on the debate that was taking place in the Christian churches, and, in direct contrast to Edward Norman, welcomed the churches' involvement in the liberation struggle.

The three approaches which have been sketched here demonstrate that there is not only diversity of opinion but a direct clash of values. The debate about South Africa has persisted in Britain for decades, becoming a touchstone of broader political commitments – an indicator of where an individual or a group stands on a range of social issues. Because of this, the concern with South Africa has become ingrained in the British domestic political debate in a way which is unusual for foreign affairs. Perhaps only Spain in the 1930s had a similar symbolic significance.

The media

The attention which the media give to South Africa illustrates this. Although the main attention comes at times of crisis and controversy, South African affairs seldom disappear from sight. A riot in South Africa can gain as much news coverage as a civil war in some other countries. The broadcasting services and the press carry regular news and features both about the Republic and more generally about southern Africa. In the twelve issues of *The Observer* between 29 October 1979 and 13 January 1980, there were 44 items on southern Africa. The main concentration was on the Zimbabwe settlement, but there were substantial items on South Africa itself. These included three pieces by Stanley Uys, a South African journalist working in London, on changes in apartheid, the black homelands, and the Broederbond; a full page in the Review section on 'The Sores of Soweto'; three longish articles on the activities of the Bureau of State Security (BOSS); and a leader on the Lions' rugby tour to the Republic. Similarly, on the radio, there have been special programmes, such as those presented by John Parry during summer 1982, covering such topics as Namibia, black trade unions and the Broederbond. Finally, the television services have screened such major programmes as Richard Dimbleby's series on the Afrikaners. Furthermore, at a time of general cutbacks in overseas correspondents, the number based in South Africa has increased. The reason is partly that the Republic can offer sophisticated communication systems, so that other parts of Africa can be covered from there, but it must also be said that – for all the criticism of the suppression of the press in South Africa – the Republic is more open to Western newsmen, their habits and style, than many black states.

Once a subject like South Africa has caught the attention of editors and correspondents, its importance tends to become self-fulfilling, and incidents related to it are regarded as 'newsworthy'. Moreover, the degree and regularity of the media coverage reinforce the sense of British involvement, and reinforce South Africa as an issue in British domestic politics. The reports are given a 'British slant' (How will it affect British trade? What will be the response of the Anti-Apartheid Movement?), which encourages the view that Britain has a special role to play in promoting change in South Africa. This has led to major pieces of investigative journalism, such as Adam Raphael's 1973 *Guardian* reports on pay and working conditions for blacks in British firms operating in South Africa, Peter Deeley's exposures of BOSS in *The Observer,* and the work of Bernard Rivers and Martin Bailey in uncovering the breaking of oil sanctions against Rhodesia.[10]

Adam Raphael's articles, which were introduced under the headline 'British firms pay Africans starvation wages', may have been exceptional in their impact, but they reveal the potential power of the media and their ability to alert and stimulate diverse British interests.[11] Not only did Raphael make the general point that some British firms were paying their black labour below the Poverty Datum Line but he named names, and famous names they were – Associated Portland Cement, Slater Walker, Tate and Lyle, Courtaulds, British Leyland, and so on. The outcry in Britain was immediate, drawing in parliament, the trade unions, the churches, the Conservative government, the whole range of the media, and, of course, the companies themselves. The companies' response was mixed. Those who had escaped criticism – like ICI, Shell and Unilever – kept quiet. Those named reacted in different ways: the chairman of Slater Walker confessed to being 'horrified' and undertook to improve the situation (which was quickly done, with a 100 per cent rise in wages of the lowest paid), whereas Tate and Lyle states that their wages 'were consistent with those in the rest of the South African sugar industry'. W. E. Luke of UKSATA stated that 'there are some British firms of whom I am not proud. But we can't tell our members what their morals should be. I would very much like to see wages increased'.[12]

The Raphael reports stimulated considerable concern in the trade unions. Leading figures like Jack Jones started to take a close interest in the development of black trade unions, while later a TUC delegation visited the Republic to investigate conditions and trade union practices. In parliament, there was the characteristic diversity of views. Some Conservatives argued that the government could have no responsibility for working conditions in the Republic, and there was mention that even lower wages were paid in places like Sri Lanka and Hong Kong. The majority reaction, however, was one of concern, and the Commons decided to investigate conditions in South Africa through the Trade and Industry Sub-Committee of the Expenditure Committee, chaired by William Rodgers. This proved to be a major undertaking, and the evidence given to the committee is encased in four volumes.[13] The committee did not, however, visit South Africa, since the South African government indicated that it would not be welcome.

The committee's evidence was reported in the press, which kept it an open issue in British politics. Some firms, such as GEC and Metal Box, undertook to improve the conditions of their black workers and to introduce bursaries and training schemes, but others argued that African labour was difficult to train and was often inefficient. After considering the evidence, the committee made a series of recommendations which were incorporated in a draft code of conduct, covering such matters as employment practice, recognition of trade unions, African training and education. It was these proposals that led a somewhat hesitant government to issue a voluntary Code of Practice for British firms operating in South Africa. This was the forerunner of the EEC Code of Conduct, and it was designed to persuade and/or pressure companies into providing better wages and working conditions for blacks. Although it was voluntary, firms were asked to publish reports, and here again the media entered the scene, for the greatest sanction behind the code was public exposure on failing to carry it out. The sequence of events, therefore, from Adam Raphael's original articles through the companies' reactions, the parliamentary investigation and the government's response, which threw the responsibility back to the companies under the threat of media exposure, exemplifies the interaction between diverse bodies, governmental and non-governmental, as well as the media's role in Britain's relationship with South Africa.

The desire to play a part in Anglo/South African relations is mirrored also in the editorial columns, where the characteristic diversity of attitudes is evident. Thus, on 22 May 1970, both the *Guardian* and *The Daily Telegraph* carried editorials on the decision of James Callaghan, the home secretary, to call on the Cricket Council to withdraw the invitation to the South African cricketers. Under the heading 'The Umpire Intervenes', the *Guardian* said, 'His decision is wise, and his reasons for it are persuasive', and saw the main issues as those of race relations and the future of the Commonwealth. However, the paper recognized that giving way to demonstrations by minority groups was 'trickier'. In contrast, the *Telegraph* leader, which was entitled 'The Demo Society', accused the home secretary of submitting to intimidation, and said that the objective of many of the demonstrators was not the cancellation of the tour or the end of apartheid 'but the overthrow of our society'. There were similar divisions of view later in the year over the sale of arms. On 21 July both papers carried leaders about a statement by the foreign secretary, Sir Alec Douglas-Home. The *Guardian* said that the Conservatives should make up their minds whether they wanted South Africa or the remainder of independent Africa as friends, for it could not be both. Any sale of arms would be seen as 'a betrayal' at the United Nations, and at best it could give only short-term benefit, for the long-term loss would be in trade with black Africa; the government should think again. In the *Telegraph*'s view, Sir Alec was acting with care and circumspection despite being surrounded by overheated reactions, including those of Harold Wilson, and it claimed that the West's military strength was its best form of influence. As for the Commonwealth, although it was to be consulted, Tanzania had already threatened to leave if arms were sold. If that were to happen, the *Telegraph* said, it 'would be their loss and not Britain's. The sooner that sinks in the better'.

The extent and diversity of media attention has, of course, implications for those involved in decision-making about the Republic. They all know that their actions may come under scrutiny, and can easily become the subject of controversy. That is true whether it is the prime minister, a senior government official, the chairman of a bank or a church leader. As a result, governments, parties and pressure groups struggle to gain sympathetic media attention; but equally the media depend on the help and contact of the political leaders and decision-makers. It is a two-way flow of mutual dependence and tension: the media anxious for access and inside views but suspicious that they may be used as a vehicle for promoting the views of others; the political leaders eager for the public prominence but fearful of unfavourable coverage.

The political parties

As far as the political parties are concerned, there is an immediate paradox. Although South Africa is frequently a topic of attention for the parties – reflecting the conflict of values and the media coverage – it has not been an election issue. This was well illustrated in 1970. In the early months of that year, there was fierce political controversy over South African sports teams visiting Britain. Characteristically, the dispute was translated into Britain's own concerns, especially the law-and-order issue which was raised by the demonstrations against the touring rugby players, and by the prospect of similar demonstrations during a cricket tour planned for the summer. When Harold Wilson announced that there would be an election in June, there was press speculation that the dispute might build into a major election isue. It did not. None of the Labour candidates mentioned it in their election addresses, and only 3 per cent of the Conservatives referred to it. Party agents were unanimous in agreeing that it had had little impact in the constituencies.[14] However, it could have been an election issue, for Harold Wilson had taken a calculated risk. While he announced on 18 May that an election would be held, it was three days later that the English cricket authorities called off the tour after considerable pressure from the government. Later he wrote: 'The Conservatives could hardly conceal their pleasure at the thought that the election campaign would take place against a background of anti-apartheid demonstrations, and that the portrayals of the resulting violence on the television screens of the nation would create a "law and order" backlash, to say nothing of the guilt by association which would adhere to the Labour Party and its leaders.'[15] Yet if that had been the case, the issue at stake would have been law and order in Britain, and not the pros and cons of links with South Africa.

The paradox of the different levels of attention given to South Africa in 1970 did not end with the election. It emerged again immediately afterwards, with the fierce political row that broke out over the new Conservative government's decision to sell arms to the Republic for 'external use'. Although the Conservatives had made clear their commitment to this before the election, it had not featured in the campaign. But when Sir Alec Douglas-Home confirmed that the government was going ahead with the sale, there was intense opposition from the Labour Party, anti-apartheid groups and the black Commonwealth states. As already noted, the South African relationship once again dominated the headlines, and when parliament assembled the Labour opposition made the arms sales one of their main points of attack.

Although the contrast between neglect at the elections and intense political activity at other times was most obvious in 1970, the relationship with South Africa has never been an election issue. There is no mention of it in the studies that were made of the two elections of 1974 and that of 1979,[16] and the only southern African topic that has come near to prominence at an election was Rhodesia in 1966, when the country went to the poll only a few months after UDI. Wilson's Labour administration was very conscious of public reaction to UDI and initially feared that the Conservatives would take advantage of the situation, but in the event Wilson gained from his handling of the crisis. Looking back some months later, Richard Crossman criticized several aspects of Wilson's behaviour, but concluded: 'I can't deny that he was moved step by step always in line with British public opinion'.[17]

What explains the paradox between electoral neglect and vigorous activity at other times? The answer may be found in the occasional public opinion surveys that have been conducted about South Africa and the British relationship. These polls have been so occasional that they cannot be used to trace long-term patterns of public attitudes, but two characteristics do stand out: first, that opinion is clearly divided; and, second, that there is a high 'don't know' response, frequently representing 20 per cent or more of those questioned. Both features create difficulties as regards making South Africa an election issue. The division of views means that the parties are unsure whether they would gain advantage by raising the matter, and the high 'don't know' response indicates that although South Africa is a matter of considerable concern to political leaders, and to those with a strong political awareness, this interest is not shared by the mass of the public, despite the amount of media attention.

The absence of a broad public concern does not imply, however, that South Africa is unimportant to the parties, even in electoral terms. The government and the opposition parties are constantly being judged by the way they handle political issues, including those like South Africa which are not the stuff of election campaigns. Kenneth Waltz has argued that in Britain there is an almost uninterrupted electoral atmosphere because the executive branch is held responsible for most actions and policies, and because of the constant speculation about the parties and their leaders. The result is that the parties are always aware and concerned about public opinion and media attention.[18] Furthermore, the political leaders see public opinion as creating a broad framework of constraints within which they have to work, setting the limits of tolerable political behaviour.

To turn to the political parties themselves, does all the attention given to the Republic by party leaders, by MPs and at party conferences add up to distinctive and consistent party attitudes to South Africa? Alongside the interest has gone dispute, both within and between the parties. Nevertheless, there are no supporters of the principle of apartheid, although some 'right-wing' Tories are accused of hypocrisy – of condemning the principle but supporting the practice. Broadly, the Conservatives have shown more inclination than the other parties to give the whites the benefit of the doubt, and to hope that if they are left alone they will 'sort things out'. In this, they are of course influenced by business interests. Many British firms with South African connections have links with the Conservative Party – including membership of their boards. For instance, in 1980 there were two major Conservative figures among the directors of Lonrho – Lord Duncan Sandys and Edward du Cann – and, before he became foreign secretary, Lord Carrington was on the RTZ board. However, there is more to it than business interests. There are 'kith and kin' feelings: for some a sense of loyalty to those whites who fought alongside Britain in two world wars, and for others the lingering ideology of imperialism with its belief in the civilizing role of the white man. It is this variety of motives that helps to explain the emergence over the years of small, inner-party groups like the Katanga and Rhodesia lobbies, and the persistence of Conservative figures like Lord Salisbury, Patrick Wall, John Biggs-Davison, Julian Amery and Rear-Admiral Morgan-Giles, who defend South Africa, or at least try to modify the criticism. Sympathy also comes from the belief among Conservatives that, because many of them have visited the Republic, they know more about it than their political opponents. Those who know South Africa well tend to present an image of a stable and moderately reforming society. When that image clashes sharply with the situation inside the Republic, as it did in 1977 with the death of Steve Biko and a wave of repression, there is confusion and disappointment in the Tory ranks. There is also plain speaking. Lord Carrington, then the leader of the Opposition in the Lords, told the South Africa Club at their 1977 London dinner that the Republic's friends were 'saddened, bewildered and horrified by Pretoria's latest spate of repression'. If the South Africans, he said, wanted the support of the West, they 'had to produce the conditions in which that support can be forthcoming amongst those of us who wish to help'.[19]

The Conservative reaction can be even sharper. The white South Africans never forget that it was a Conservative prime minister who, in their eyes, helped to direct the wind of change against them, and a similar tough Conservative message came in 1981 when Edward Heath, the former prime minister, told a Johannesburg audience that, 'unless and until the dismantlement of apartheid is assured, it would be a grave mistake for South Africa to base her strategy on the assumption that when the chips are down the West will stand with her'. He described the reforms that had taken place as not 'even remotely adequate', and stressed that there could be no satisfactory solution short of some form of universal franchise at the national level. He concluded by saying that the lesson of history was that the more black nationalist movements were suppressed, the more they would 'resort to violence, to extremist ideologies and to the patronage of radical or anti-Western nations'.[20] In Britain, Heath's speech raised angry reactions from some Conservatives, the *Daily Telegraph* leader calling it 'mistaken and unwise'.

Heath's remarks (and the reactions to them) illustrate the conflict that arises inside a party where sympathy for the whites coexists with disillusionment about their reforming claims, and even strong opposition to the structure of white dominance. This internal party tension appeared during the arms sales debates, and even more clearly over Rhodesia's UDI and the imposition of economic sanctions. As one observer wrote, for the Conservatives 'Rhodesia was a bedevilled question. Wherever Heath positioned himself, opposition sprang up somewhere in the party.'[21] And the problem persisted each year as the order for the renewal of sanctions came before parliament. Between 1965 and 1979, 120 Conservative MPs defied their leaders by voting against it on one or more occasions, and 21 of them voted four or more times against it. In 1972, on the day before the sanctions legislation was to be debated, a letter opposing it appeared in *The Times* signed by 42 Conservative backbenchers. Despite Sir Alec Douglas-Home urging support for continuing sanctions, and a two-line government whip, 31 Conservatives voted against the sanctions order and more than 70 were absent. The Conservative government was able to carry its sanctions policy only because it had the support of the Labour and Liberal parties.[22] While that defiance of the leadership came from the right wing, there have also been worries on the other side of the party. At the beginning of the Heath administration in 1970, a group of 40 MPs openly expressed their concern about the sale of arms to the Republic.[23]

Divisions over southern Africa have been even more pronounced at Conservative Party conferences. Throughout the 1970s there were constant disputes about Rhodesia, and a particularly bitter incident took place at the 1978 conference. John Davies, the shadow foreign secretary, who had just returned from an African trip, criticized the Labour government's handling of Rhodesia, but he went on to emphasize that a settlement could be achieved only with the agreement of the majority of the people of Rhodesia and the support of the neighbouring black states.

Davies failed to persuade many of the delegates. Instead he was faced by demands for the lifting of sanctions, and the recognition of the recently formed Smith/Muzorewa administration, which many Conservatives believed satisfied the principles that Britain had been seeking to achieve. Part of Davies's problems can be attributed to the poor presentation of his speech. Unknown to the delegates, he was a dying man and this was to be his last speech. Not surprisingly, he was faltering and hesitant, and throughout the speech there was hissing, stamping of feet and cat calls from the floor, but the presentation only partly explains the opposition; the main cause lay in the divisions among Conservatives.[24]

The Labour Party's strong stand against apartheid has become a symbol of its opposition to racism everywhere, but on occasions this deep and genuine commitment has also served to unite the party by distancing it from the Tories. The unity on South African issues has been clearer in opposition – when the party has been able to rally round a great cause, without the constraints of office, which have sometimes led to divisions. The divisions have not simply reflected rifts between the right and the left wings, for some of the most active opponents of apartheid have been drawn from the 'right' (such as David Owen and Reg Prentice, when they were in the party) and the 'centre' (such as Bob Hughes and Frank Hooley).

The fiercest and most public of the Labour divisions was the 1967 cabinet dispute over the sale of arms to South Africa. The dispute was both about the decision itself, and about the way it was handled. George Brown, who was foreign secretary at the time, later complained of 'the extraordinary lengths' to which Harold Wilson, the prime minister, had gone 'not merely to bow to the feelings of the party on the arms issue but . . . to organize the feelings of the party'.[25] When, in 1969, the arms sales question was raised again, some ministers, despite the bitter division of two years earlier, again pressed for the resumption of sales. Both sides claimed that if their advice was not followed there would be disastrous political consequences – one side stressing the job opportunities that would be created by new arms orders, the other saying that such a step would be so unpopular in the party that it would split it apart and divide the cabinet from its followers inside and outside parliament. According to Richard Crossman, when the Chief Whip was consulted about backbench reaction, his advice was clear: 'To sell them [the arms] will cause a disaster in the party'. There was, wrote Crossman, no further discussion.[26]

Divisions among Labour members have also been apparent on the issue of trade. In May 1970, Harold Wilson, under question in the Commons, said that whereas the arms ban had been strictly imposed, there had never been any doubt that 'we wish to increase trade in peaceful conditions'.[27] Two months later, however, when the Labour Party had lost power, Judith Hart, who had been a member of the previous government, speculated about the damage of continuing trade with the Republic: 'We must look very closely at whether we believe we can cooperate further with...a country which persecutes, which is oppressive, which is racialist... which is, in fact the most vivid embodiment of fascism that we know in the world today.'[28] Despite that, the party in opposition soon rallied together. At the party conference in the autumn of that year, representatives of the black nationalist parties – 'comrades in the liberation movements in southern Africa', as they were described – were present to hear Harold Wilson bring the hall to life by denouncing both the proposed sale of arms and the Conservatives' attempts to gain a Rhodesian settlement. On Rhodesia, he accused the Tory leadership of appeasing a racist regime to keep their own extremists in the party's ranks. 'History will not forgive them', he declared, 'nor shall we tolerate a settlement based on the racialist principles of the police state.'[29]

In power, however, the signs of strain have been clear. The structure of the Labour Party, with its alternative centres of power – the parliamentary party, the National Executive Council (NEC), the annual conference, and the trade unions – tends to expose the divisions. In 1974, for example, the NEC led an attack upon the Labour government for allowing naval exercises with the South Africans. In this, it was strongly supported by the party conference, where a resolution was passed affirming that the NEC, as the custodian of the party's policies between annual conferences, had rightly opposed the exercises. Characteristically, the conference gave particular support for those ministers on the NEC who had adopted a radical approach. In this case it was Judith Hart, Joan Lestor and Tony Benn. Joan Lestor, who was then a junior minister at the Foreign Office, joined the criticism of the government, urging the conference delegates not only to support the motion, but to help end the 1955 Simonstown Agreement. She said that even if trade links had to be kept, there was no excuse for retaining military contacts.[30] The resolution was overwhelmingly approved, and this may have started the process by which the Labour government withdrew from the Simonstown Agreement in the following year.

There was no respite for the Labour government from conference pressure. In 1976 a resolution was carried calling for an immediate freeze on all new investment to South Africa, and the breaking of all links by nationalized companies and banks. In 1979 the conference called for mandatory sanctions against South Africa, and for legislation to prevent new investments and to cut economic, cultural and sporting links. Joan Lestor was again prominent, this time speaking for the NEC. 'If you don't want to see large-scale war in South Africa', she said, 'then you have to take seriously the question of economic sanctions.'[31]

Labour's conviction that the party has a special responsibility to show compassion to the underprivileged is combined with the belief that if greater racial justice cannot be achieved in southern Africa, then there is a real threat of increased racial friction at home and elsewhere abroad. In such matters, the Labour Party has no faith in the Conservatives – that they understand and care either about justice and equality, or about the consequences of white dominance in southern Africa. Michael Foot made that clear when speaking to the Tribune Group on the eve of the party's 1978 conference. In explaining the Labour government's decision to delay the election – a delay that many party members opposed – the main reasons he gave were international, and the situation in southern Africa in particular. He believed that affairs there were 'coming to a crisis', and he picked out for special mention the emergence of a new government in South Africa, the South African rejection of proposals for a Namibian settlement and the continuing Rhodesian problem. In handling these affairs he underlined the importance of having a Labour government in power.[32] Although there must be doubt that southern African affairs featured as prominently in the government's election calculations as Foot suggested, the fact that he was willing to give them such public emphasis indicates the importance the party attaches to them. By 1982, as party leader, he was prepared to state that when Labour returned to power, it would support mandatory economic sanctions against the Republic, and the party came out in open support of the black liberation movements.

Of all the parties the Liberals have had the most unified attitude to southern Africa – vigorously opposing apartheid and white minority rule. In parliament they faithfully voted for sanctions and against the sale of arms; in conference they have regularly passed anti-apartheid resolutions, and they have put sustained pressure on the government of the day to oppose racism. Liberals have been prominent in the Anti-Apartheid Movement, with Jeremy Thorpe and David Steel having held office in the organization. For much of the 1970s the Young Liberals were so much at the forefront of the anti-apartheid campaign that their leader, the South African exile Peter Hain, tried to use that section of the party as a vehicle to pressure the government into a more radical stance against the Republic. In the South Africa debate, therefore, the party has been more important than the size of its parliamentary representation would suggest.

Of course the Liberals have enjoyed the relatively uncomplicated position of being able to express their abhorrence of apartheid without the constraints which come from holding office. Yet even among the Liberals there have been signs of tension: the militant views, and even more the militant methods, of the Young Liberals were opposed by many of the older members of the party, who felt that the YL leaders were using the party exclusively as a vehicle for anti-apartheid activities. Had the Liberals ever held office, another potential source of division might have been the conflict between their sympathy for the blacks as an oppressed group and their commitment to the rights of individuals and minorities, including the whites. There were signs of this at the 1977 conference, when a motion by Paul Hammond deploring the support given by British interests to 'the repressive white regimes in Rhodesia and South Africa' was carried without opposition, to be followed by an amendment by Roger Pincham (which also went through unopposed) calling for the protection of minority rights – including those of whites – after universal franchise has been achieved in southern Africa.[33] So far the Liberals have not had the problem of reconciling different principles. Whether that position will change in an alliance with the Social Democratic Party is an unknown, but what seems clear is that the SDP, with leaders like David Owen in its ranks, will be no less committed against apartheid than the Liberals have been on their part.

5 Pressure Groups

The groups in Britain which are most closely involved in South African affairs can be divided into three categories. First, there are the anti-apartheid groups, such as the Anti-Apartheid Movement (AAM), the Defence and Aid Fund (D and AF) and the South African Non-Racial Olympic Committee (SANROC). These are 'promotional groups', intent on forwarding their cause – the elimination of apartheid. They have a radical image, and their main links are with the left of British politics. They have no official status, but they are not necessarily excluded from the British government and they have good access to international organizations. Second, there are business and financial groups, which are made up of those who have strong economic links with the Republic. They seek to guard existing interests and to foster future relations. They also show concern for Western security, and they fear the spread of communism. Their main links are with the right wing of British politics; they have an establishment image, and work within government and business structures, often enjoying good relations with government officials. The third group is made up of bodies with wider interests and membership – like the British Council of Churches and the Trades Union Congress – but in which South African issues are regularly raised. These groups help to integrate the issues further into British political activity by linking them to a broad range of interests.

Although a distinction has been drawn between the 'radical' and the 'establishment' images of the groups, the contrast should be treated with caution. Opposition to apartheid is widespread in British society, and a highly committed promotional group like the Anti-Apartheid Movement has been able to draw its support from the Labour and Liberal parties, the churches, the universities and the trade unions. When Labour administrations have been in power, and especially when Dr David Owen was foreign secretary, anti-apartheid groups have had good access to government. Their acceptance is even clearer in the international setting, where they form part of a radical 'establishment' which is supported by the black governments and officials from international organizations. Indeed the anti-apartheid groups often provide the information and ideas on which the international organizations act against South Africa.

Another feature of the anti-apartheid groups is the role of the political exiles. Although their numbers are not great, they compensate for that by their commitment and energy, and they have helped to transfer part of the South African struggle to Britain. SANROC, for example, was established in South Africa in 1962–3, but when its leaders, Dennis Brutus and Chris de Broglio, were forced out of South Africa, they re-formed SANROC in Britain, since when it has operated from London. Yet although the exiles are important to the pressure groups and often provide the drive that might otherwise be missing, they would count for little if the movement against apartheid did not have substantial support from British people.

A final general point to note is the change in the methods and attitudes of the promotional groups, reflecting changes in attitudes towards South Africa both internationally and in Britain. Before 1960 the British groups tended to be small and to support peaceful reform – to assume 'the inevitability of gradualism'. Then in the early 1960s, following the shooting at Sharpeville and the flight to Britain of many political refugees, larger and more vigorous anti-apartheid groups were formed, attitudes became harder and tactics more militant. In the late 1960s and early 1970s another wave of protests was generated, this time linked to the broader movement in the West against authority and established institutions, and in Britain this became linked to the South African issue. Radical and student groups put it high on their agenda, protesting through public demonstrations, sit-ins at universities and colleges, pressure on investors, banks and business concerns, and by giving their support to anti-apartheid groups. By the late 1970s that period was over. Even the Soweto riots did not bring out mass demonstrations. However, the protest against South Africa was not over – it had simply entered a new phase. South Africa remained firmly on the political agenda, for one of the great triumphs of the anti-apartheid groups had been to politicize all contacts with the Republic, and to entrench concern with South Africa in the British public conscience.

The Anti-Apartheid Movement (AAM)

The work and effectiveness of the pressure groups is best understood by looking at particular examples. The largest of the groups that campaign against the South African government is the Anti-Apartheid Movement. Its origins lie in the call from the African National Congress (ANC) of South Africa at the All-Africa Peoples' Conference in 1958 for a boycott of South African goods. In Britain a Boycott Movement was launched at a mass rally in Trafalgar Square in February 1960, addressed by Father Trevor Huddleston and Julius Nyerere. Shortly afterwards came the killings at Sharpeville, and the movement decided to extend its activities to total opposition to South Africa's racial policies. To achieve that, a new organization was formed – the Anti-Apartheid Movement.[1]

Although the organization was founded in Britain, it is now international. Its aims are to inform the public about apartheid and its implications in South Africa; to campaign for action to bring apartheid to an end; and to cooperate with other organizations working against apartheid.[2] While the broad aims have remained constant, the role of the movement has changed with circumstances. For example, during the period between the arrest of the ANC leaders at Rivonia in 1962 and the Soweto riots of 1976, when the South African government succeeded in suppressing much of the internal black opposition, one of the AAM's main tasks was to keep the cause alive by organizing international pressure on Pretoria. After the Soweto riots and the revival of the ANC (both inside and outside South Africa), the AAM was able to give more emphasis to support for black South African political movements. The AAM's tactics inside Britain have also responded to mood and circumstance. The great demonstrations against the rugby tourists in 1969–70 were appropriate for that time, but by the late 1970s and early 1980s the AAM's hope was to exercise more precise political pressure through parties and the government.

At any one time the AAM may concentrate on a number of specific campaigns. Over the years, certain issues have recurred: the campaign against arms sales, support for 'political prisoners', opposition to British investment and sporting and cultural ties, and pressure for economic sanctions. The AAM leaders believe that concentration on precise aims has paid dividends. For instance, they believe that campaigns on behalf of arrested black nationalists have in some cases transformed death penalties into prison sentences; they also believe that they made a significant contribution to the UN mandatory arms ban. The movement had been campaigning for this for years, but even in the months immediately before the ban was imposed they were told by David Owen, then foreign secretary, that it was not practical politics. The Soweto riots of 1976 changed that. In the outburst of indignation which followed, Britain and other Western states which had previously resisted the ban wanted to demonstrate their opposition to apartheid. The arms ban was at hand, for the AAM had kept it in the forefront of attention and done the groundwork for its implementation. The politicians seized it.

By 1979 the British movement had a membership of 2,790, of whom the great bulk were individual members (2,450), but the smaller number of affiliated members – such as trade unions, branches of political parties and student unions – gave the AAM links with a much larger pool of supporters. The number of associated members has grown steadily – from 115 in 1975 to 340 by 1979 – and particular stress has been laid on increasing trade union support.[3] The 1979–80 report did not give total membership numbers, but said that of the 90 organizations that had affiliated that year 40 were trade unions.[4] The number of individual members has remained reasonably steady over the years, with a core of people who retain membership, but also an annual turnover of several hundreds. For its finances, the movement depends on members' subscriptions, special appeals and functions, and contributions from sympathetic individuals and organizations, but although much of the AAM's work has been undertaken by unpaid volunteers, there have been regular financial problems. So far the shortfall from subscriptions has been overcome by special grants from such organizations as the World Council of Churches, the Rowntree Trust and the Defence and Aid Fund, as well as some trade union support.

AAM has a characteristic organizational framework, with a large national committee, from which a smaller executive committee is drawn, and a central office manned by full-time staff. In addition there are committees to coordinate activities with other organizations, and there are local branches throughout the country. According to the annual reports, the number of branches is never static – 38 in 1975, 62 in 1979 and back to 45 in 1980 – some groups disappearing, others being established, yet others being reactivated. Local activity tends to be patchy. As the 1979–80 report admitted: 'The creation of a genuinely national spread of local anti-apartheid activities and groups remains an unfulfilled, and crucial, objective of the AAM if it is to continue to be an effective *movement* rather than a London-based pressure group with occasional support from elsewhere.'[5] The central organization tries to retain regular contact with the branches, through correspondence and the circulation of *Anti-Apartheid News*, the movement's newspaper. In their turn, the branches use the newspaper to advertise their activities and seek support. In an attempt to overcome communication problems, a Scottish coordinating committee was established in 1977, and in 1980 a new member of the headquarters staff was appointed with special responsibility for local groups (and also for contact with the trade unions).

The range of support for the AAM is reflected in the diverse settings in which it has promoted its cause – church services at Westminster Abbey and St Martin-in-the-Fields, Trades Union Congresses, student unions, mass rallies in Trafalgar Square, combined public meetings with the African National Congress. As already noted, although the great majority of members are British, South African exiles have played an important part in building the AAM, especially in the early days. These exiles include Ethel de Keyser, a past secretary of the movement, and the present honorary secretary, Abdul Minty. However, over the years the balance has shifted so that British officials and executive members now predominate.

The movement has links with all three main political parties in Britain, and with the small British Communist Party. Even among the Conservatives there is some contact through the Reform Group and the Conservative Students, but there are few Tory members. Support for the movement comes predominantly from the left, where the ties with the Labour Party have been especially useful. Prominent Labour figures who have been members of the AAM, like Barbara Castle, John Ennals, Joan Lestor and Bob Hughes, have held government office, and have not been afraid to exert pressure inside the government against South Africa. Barbara Castle, for instance, was a determined opponent in government of the sale of arms to the Republic, and an equally determined supporter of sanctions against Rhodesia. In addition, the AAM staff has regular contact with Labour and Liberal party headquarters, and AAM representatives attend party conferences, where they encourage the introduction of anti-apartheid resolutions on the conference floor. The AAM also has had meetings with, and is used as a source of information by, the Parliamentary Labour Party's Africa Committee, which reports to the party's International Committee. Yet despite these strong ties, the AAM has often been critical of the Labour Party in office, on the grounds that it has not been sufficiently militant.

The political status achieved by the AAM, both in Britain and internationally, is reflected in the prominence and diversity of the speakers it can attract for its meetings. A conference in London in March 1982, called 'Southern Africa: The Time to Choose', which was largely concerned with exerting pressure for mandatory economic sanctions against the Republic, was addressed by party leaders Michael Foot and David Steel; a representative of the British trade unions – Tom Jackson; representatives of African states – the vice-president of Nigeria and the foreign minister of the Seychelles; major officials of international organizations – the chairman of the UN Anti-Apartheid Committee, and the secretary-general of the Commonwealth Secretariat; representatives of the black nationalist movements – both from the ANC and from SWAPO; and, finally, the AAM leaders – Bob Hughes the Labour MP, who chaired the conference, Trevor Huddleston, the president of the movement, and Abdul Minty, the honorary secretary. Yet despite the prominence of the contributors, there was a flaw: those who would be responsible for imposing economic sanctions – the Conservative government and the business community – were not represented. However distinguished, therefore, it was a conference of those who were seeking to exert pressure rather than those who took the decisions.

The AAM has also formed and supported smaller groups. The proliferation of these and their initials – CANUC (The Campaign Against the Namibian Uranium Contract), COSAWR (The Committee of South African War Resisters, i.e. young whites who oppose military service), SATIS (South Africa – The Imprisoned Society) – is bewildering.

However, they increase the effectiveness of the organization, because the small groups can concentrate on specific issues and can give a greater number of people the opportunity to feel commitment, to take initiatives and to avoid being lost in a large organization. Some of the groups are created for special circumstances, such as the Stop the Seventies Tour (STST) and the Zimbabwe Emergency Campaign Committee (ZECC), which the AAM helped to form when the Conservatives were returned to power in 1979. Other groups with particular purposes have indefinite time-scales. These include SANROC, End Loans to South Africa, COSAWR, and the World Campaign Against Military and Nuclear Collaboration with South Africa, which was launched in London in March 1979 by the AAM and the United Nations Centre Against Apartheid, with the intention of resisting the West's support for 'a nuclear Frankenstein in Africa'. The founding patrons of the campaign were Presidents Kaunda of Zambia, Khama of Botswana and Nyerere of Tanzania, and its sponsors included Olof Palme of Sweden, Joan Lestor and David Steel. Its secretary is Abdul Minty. The importance of AAM in coordinating anti-apartheid work was demonstrated during Anti-Apartheid Year (April 1978–March 1979), when a special secretary, funded by a Foreign Office grant, was based at AAM headquarters.[6]

There are two segments of British society in which support for the movement has been less than anticipated. These are the trade unions and the black community. From the beginning the AAM identified the unions as a major potential ally and has persistently sought their support through a joint TUC/AAM coordinating committee, through regular attendance at TUC conferences, through special 'action weeks', and through the affiliation of unions and union branches. These activities have borne some fruit. The AAM's position on South Africa is regularly endorsed at TUC conferences, an increasing number of unions have become affiliated, individual leaders like Jack Jones and Tom Jackson have been prominent supporters, and there has been local trade union action initiated by AAM contacts. In 1976, for instance, following the banning of 23 trade union organizers in South Africa, there was action in several parts of the country. Yet, despite some successes and increasing official union support, the movement has had little impact on rank-and-file members. This was recognized in the 1977–8 annual report, which said: 'The achievements were, taken as a whole, modest and it was clear that many trade unionists do not accept all aspects of AAM policy, especially the need to isolate South Africa economically.'[7] The effort continues, however, and by the early 1980s the AAM leadership felt that it was making progress, since the TUC passed a resolution supporting sanctions at its 1981 conference, and a TUC representative (Tom Jackson) was appointed to attend the AAM rally in March 1982.

Among the British black population there has been even less impact. According to the 1977–8 annual report, some black newspapers had carried AAM reports, ties had been strengthened with some Community Relations Councils, and activities had been organized with other anti-racist groups, such as the Anti-Nazi League, but there was no wide response.[8] The report for the following year stressed that 'this area of the AAM's work . . . requires much closer attention in the future', but the 1979–80 report recorded little progress. It noted some developments, including efforts by local branches to involve black groups, but generally it concluded: 'The level of support for the AAM from the black community has not changed significantly in the past year . . . It remains the case that the AAM's work does not make a significant or lasting impression on either the West Indian or Asian communities.'[9]

Because the AAM draws its support from such a variety of sources, its activities and allegiances can be interpreted in a variety of ways. For some, the emphasis is put on its links with radical organizations, and communists in particular.[10] Certainly the AAM does have that support. Its viewpoint has been advanced through communist publications like *Socialist Challenge* and *Socialist Worker*, and it has backing from the British and the South African Communist parties, the latter having links with the African National Congress. Some critics therefore conclude that the AAM is a tool for communism, and that the non-communists who support it are naive dupes. That is far too narrow an interpretation. Although it has communist support and cooperates with the ANC, it is not a mere tool or cover for either. An alternative interpretation is to put the AAM in the tradition of the great causes for liberal and humanitarian aims – like the Anti-Slavery Movement. From this standpoint a diversity of people, with a variety of political views on other issues, are brought together in opposition to racism and the injustice shown to the blacks of South Africa.

In fact, no single ideological label can be applied to the AAM's members. There are those who base their stand on Christian conviction, others (Christian and non-Christian) who see the situation in terms of individual human rights, and many who are simply expressing a strong concern against any form of racial discrimination. However, having recognized that, a broad ideological approach can be traced in AAM literature which represents an important, but not representative, stream of opinion within the movement. This has a strong left-wing slant in which apartheid is associated with capitalism, and the treatment of the blacks in South Africa with a broader framework of global exploitation. The main instruments are seen to be the Western multinational companies, which have the support of their home government – even if this is sometimes limited to benign tolerance of the companies' activities. Within this capitalist structure, South Africa not only is the recipient of support, but is itself the base from which capitalism is spreading its control across the whole subcontinent. Britain's particular contribution to the situation is traced to its colonial past, and Britain's stake in apartheid remains through the economic links which are fostered by the companies with the encouragement of the government.[11]

As an organization orientated to action, the AAM's primary aims are to mobilize public opinion and to act as a check on governments and companies. Although AAM literature claims that the movement seeks support from a large section of the British public, it does not advocate policies of consensus or compromise. This explains the AAM's response to Adam Raphael's reports on working conditions in British companies in South Africa. The reports themselves were welcomed, but the reformist response, urging incremental change through internal reform and the use of economic links as a means of such reform, was condemned. The AAM view was that, 'once any campaign against discriminatory wage policies is conducted within the limits of this "change through internal reform" perspective, it can be seen as one attempting *to prevent a real restructuring* of the South African political and economic system and one calculated *to divert attention . . . from the liberation struggle*' (italics mine).[12] In short, although there is no single ideology, much AAM literature rests on a world-view in which Western capitalism is the main external prop of the apartheid system and the South African government. In AAM eyes that government, as well as oppressing the blacks within the country, is intent on dominating its neighbours in the subcontinent, by force of arms if necessary.[13]

In addition to *Anti-Apartheid News*, the AAM publishes annual reports, pamphlets and special reports. Some of its most effective publishing has been in cooperation with other organizations. Internationally, the UN Centre Against Apartheid has regularly released AAM literature, and an example of cooperation in Britain was the 1978 booklet *Shell and BP in South Africa*, written by Martin Bailey and published jointly by the AAM and the Haselmere Group, a small group of radical journalists. The AAM view has also found outlets in full-length studies, including some in the Penguin African series, which is edited by Ronald Segal, an exiled South African. Among the Penguin titles are *The South African Connection*, written by Ruth First, Jonathan Steel and Christabel Gurney (then editor of *Anti-Apartheid News*), and *Sanctions Against South Africa*, which Segal himself edited, and which consisted of the papers from a conference jointly sponsored by the AAM and the ANC.

One of the great strengths of the AAM is its persistence. The movement's activities are characterized by regular, steady pressure. The campaign launched against Barclays Bank in 1970 was noted in the

1978–9 report as being still 'one of the most popular in this field', with the National Union of Students (NUS) planning to continue it.[14] Similarly, a joint AAM/NUS effort against university investment in South Africa was launched in 1976 following inquiries into the investment patterns of 60 top companies. Under repeated pressure, some universities, including Bath and Warwick, decided to disinvest, and there were deep divisions elsewhere. The same persistence characterized the AAM's campaign against the sale of arms to South Africa. When the UN mandatory ban was imposed in November 1977, following the Soweto riots and the death of Steve Biko, the AAM's long campaign had succeeded in its immediate goal, but characteristically the AAM did not leave it at that. The movement immediately geared itself to ensure that the ban was tightly implemented. In December, Abdul Minty, the AAM secretary, addressed a special meeting of the UN Special Committee on Apartheid, detailing fourteen areas of continued military collaboration, and there was separate pressure on the British government. In March 1978, an AAM delegation met Mr Ted Rowlands, the minister of state at the FCO, to discuss the embargo and to raise complaints about the way it was being implemented. When the government's Orders in Council were published, covering some aspects of the ban, the AAM called a press conference to criticize them.

In AAM eyes no form of contact with South Africa is too small to be irrelevant. A few examples from the activities of local groups will serve to illustrate this. In 1973 the South London branch picketed local super-markets selling South African products. In 1975 the Croydon group called on the home secretary to withdraw the passports of Eric Sykes and Jimmy Edwards for entertaining Rhodesian troops. In the same year the Glasgow AAM persuaded the local authority not to purchase any South African goods, picketed performances of the musical *Ipi Tombi*, and infiltrated meetings of the Springbok Association. In 1978–9 the Southampton branch waged a successful campaign against the local police sending cadets for training in South Africa. The list goes on. To repeat the point, there is no contact with South Africa that the AAM believes can or should be ignored. Its activities in London are geared in particular for public attention – from rallies in Trafalgar Square, and vigils outside the South African Embassy, through church services, marches, the disruption of shareholders' meetings, and anti-apartheid banners on public monuments. Some of the demonstrations are held regularly, such as South Africa's Freedom Day on 26 June; others are organized in response to particular developments, or as part of special campaigns, as in Anti-Apartheid Year. In the age of public protest the AAM has been a vanguard movement.

In many ways the AAM has been an effective pressure group, but, as with the black states in the international setting, its greatest effectiveness may be in its long-term influence. The long-term effect has not necessarily been built up evenly. Major incidents like Sharpeville and the Soweto riots have seen great surges of sympathy for the South African blacks on which the AAM and other anti-apartheid groups have been able to build, but even these bursts are best seen as part of a steady shift in public attitudes.

The business community

Before we turn to the two main business groups which are specifically concerned with South Africa – the South Africa Foundation and UKSATA – mention should be made of the multinational companies whose activities have been special targets for anti-apartheid attack. In one sense all British companies operating in South Africa are multinational, but the greatest criticism is levelled at giants like ICI, Unilever, RTZ, BP, Shell and GEC. Although the multinationals, like other participants in international relations, are subject to powerful constraints, their wealth, organization and ability to operate across state boundaries give them a considerable degree of independence. This can become critical in such sensitive areas as southern Africa, where governments are anxious to retain oversight of the activities of their business companies. In Britain's case, this was demonstrated in the breaking of Rhodesian oil sanctions. Five oil companies were involved, including BP and Shell. The British government may not have known of this immediately after Rhodesia's UDI, but it certainly knew within a couple of years, and yet it turned a blind eye, neither implementing its own legislation nor carrying out the UN Security Council's resolutions. Whether the government could have prevented the oil reaching Rhodesia is an open question, but what is not in dispute is that it never really tried. A conspiracy theory has been advanced in which the government and the companies are said to have been united in their efforts to uphold the white regime, whatever the government's public claims might be.[15] What seems more probable, however, is that there was a difference of interests between the government and the companies on the sanctions issue, but the government had other interests and priorities which it was not prepared to risk in confrontation with the companies.

Whatever the reasons, the incident emphasizes the degree of autonomy enjoyed by oil companies. They circumvented sanctions under different legal regimes, and could therefore claim that they were not breaking the law. Since it was the branches of the companies in the Republic which supplied the oil, the multinationals were able to argue that they had no choice: they were obeying the laws of the country in which they operated. It is not surprising that in 1973 a South African newspaper stated: 'There can be no greater blessing for South Africa – apart from the fact that Iran is well disposed – than that the oil business is still largely in the hands of international companies with no discernible leanings of excessive patriotism.'[16] Since that time the Iranian connection has disappeared, but not the oil companies.

The South Africa Foundation

The South Africa Foundation is a South African organization established in 1959. Its main aims are to strengthen international ties, and to improve South Africa's international relations, especially with the West and especially in economic matters. The Foundation is a non-governmental body, which enjoys the support of prominent individual South Africans, but its main backing comes from the business community. It boasts the support of 80 per cent of the Republic's leading mining, industrial and commercial firms. There are a few Asians and Africans on the board of trustees, but its membership is overwhelmingly white. It draws support from both the Afrikaner and the English business communities, but its roots and style reflect the strong English tradition in South African business and industry.

Overseas the Foundation has four offices – in London, Bonn, Paris and Washington. The London office has a small staff under a director, currently Mr Roy Macnab, who has held the post through the 1970s. In some respects, its activities in Britain overlap with those of the South African Embassy, and there are close contacts between the two, but the Foundation insists on the independence of its operation. It also sees itself as non-political. This claim is based on the fact that it is not tied to a particular political party, receives no government funds, and is prepared to criticize aspects of the South African government's policies. However, if the South African situation is seen as one in which the core of the problem is a conflict between those who are defending an established structure and those seeking to overthrow that structure, by revolution if necessary, then the Foundation is a very political organization. The AAM has no doubts on this score, identifying the Foundation as 'the most important lobbying machinery' for those in Britain who are determined to strengthen ties with the apartheid regime.[17] The Foundation's own statement of aims underlines this broad political orientation. It claims that there is a lack of international understanding of South Africa which 'is exacerbated by the widespread existence of well-organized groups and individuals' who attempt to isolate the Republic. It sees its function as informing businessmen and politicians both of the cost of isolating South Africa (including the adverse effect that would have on social progress inside the country) and of the Republic's strategic importance, particularly its mineral wealth.[18]

The Foundation's ambiguous attitude to a 'political' position emerges even in the speeches of its leaders. In his 1971 presidential address Sir

Francis de Guingand stated that when the Foundation was established an undertaking was given to keep it non-political, for 'to have taken a party-political stance would have split our organization from top to bottom'. Yet later he said that he made no excuse for touching on 'the political scene, for it is politics ... which dominate our relations with other countries in the world today'.[19] With that acceptance of the importance of politics, there is no doubt that the Foundation's sympathies lie with conservative governments in the West. Thus, in the 1980 presidential address, Mr W.F. de la Harpe Beck noted with approval the 'perceptible shift towards the right in many Western countries', especially in the USA, and in Britain the friendlier atmosphere since Mrs Thatcher's administration came into power.[20] Moreover, the Foundation makes no attempt to gain mass support, or to draw public attention to itself. It concentrates on top-level contacts, mainly among businessmen, politicians, those in the media and academics. Thus, in the field of journalism, listed among those with whom it had contacts during 1978–9 were the editors of *The Sunday Times* and the *Telegraph*, the foreign editors of *The Times* and the *Daily Express*, and the chairman of Reuters and of the *Observer*. The contrast between the Foundation and the AAM is a sharp one: while the AAM draws in a strong infusion of youth to support vigorous public campaigning, the Foundation moves largely outside the public eye, among a band of establishment figures.

Since one of the Foundation's chief roles is to facilitate contacts between Britain and South Africa, and since this is a two-way flow, the Foundation has, perhaps to its surprise, found itself not only presenting 'the true image' of South Africa abroad, but conveying back to South Africa other countries' views of the Republic. De Guingand recognized this in his 1971 speech, admitting that the Foundation's task had been made more difficult because 'certain apsects of our policies run counter to present world trends'. He appealed to the South African government to change such policies as job reservation. 'I, like many others,' he said, 'find this policy very difficult to defend.'[21] A similar message came in Mr Basil Hersov's presidential address in 1978. He spoke of a dark period for South Africa, following the Soweto riots and Steve Biko's death, and emphasized that there was 'a desperate need for South Africa to do something to help its friends defend their friendship'.[22]

The outcome is that the Foundation has become a supporter of the 'change through contact' argument, according to which, from Britain's point of view, contacts, as well as being beneficial, promote reform in the Republic, and from South Africa's point of view, reforms are necessary in order to retain vital international links. The emphasis differs among Foundation members, some supporting reform because they reject the discriminatory policies, others reluctantly accepting it to retain international

links. Whatever the motives, by 1980 the Foundation was openly emphasizing its two-way role, whereby it not only provided information about
South Africa, but reported back in order 'to engender a responsible and
sophisticated reaction...amongst South Africans themselves'.[23] It also
recruited 'liberal' employees like David Willers, who shortly after his
appointment called for the release of Nelson Mandela, 'as a symbol of the
government's determination to effect reconciliation between the races'.[24]
Also in 1980 Peter Sorour, the Foundation's director-general, said: 'We
have appealed for internal actions also to be assessed for their external
effects. For example, withdrawing the passports of known opponents of
the government gives credence to our police-state image;...aggressive
posturing towards a still unformed Zimbabwe government compares
poorly with Mr Mugabe's calm statesmanship which has immeasurably
enhanced his stature in the world circles.'[25] While there have been changes
of emphasis in the Foundation's approach, such as the reformist burst of
the 1980s, its basic message, as revealed in its monthly newspaper *The
South Africa Foundation News* and its quarterly journal *South Africa International*, has four main strands: that South Africa is misunderstood
overseas; that the economy is strong; that incremental reform is desirable;
that 'responsible' overseas views have to be heeded.

As regards the British political parties, the Foundation's strongest links
are with the Conservatives, and that influences the degree of access it has
to government. Shortly before Mrs Thatcher came to power, the
Foundation's annual report recorded that: 'Frequent contact was
maintained with the Conservative Research Centre...The President and
the London Director called on Sir Keith Joseph, MP, head of the Conservative Party Policy Centre, and the Director-General spoke to a group of
MPs...Personal contacts were extended to include some shadow
ministers as well as the new Shadow Foreign Secretary, Francis Pym.'[26]
These contacts bore fruit when the Conservatives were in office. However,
contact with Labour administrations has not been altogether absent.
When Basil Hersov visited Britain in 1978, he was received 'with great
friendliness' by Lord Goronwy-Roberts, the minister of state at the
Foreign Office. Speaking later in the House of Lords, Goronwy-Roberts
said that 'perhaps it is by the pressure of connection rather than of dis-
connection that we can hope to influence the situation in areas like South
Africa.'[27]

An important aspect of the Foundation's work is the visits it arranges
between South Africa and Britain. Each year it sponsors a number of
prominent Britons to visit the Republic, and helps many more by
arranging itineraries, contacts and interviews when they are there. In
reverse it helps South African visitors to Britain. In South Africa its main
links are with the white community, but it also arranges meetings with

'moderate' black leaders. The 1980–1 report showed that recent visitors had had interviews with such prominent blacks as Chief Gatsha Butelezi (chief minister of Kwazulu), Dr N. Motlana (chairman of the Soweto Committee of Ten), Mr D. Thebahali (chairman of the Soweto Council) and Mr Percy Qoboza (editor of *The Post*). In Britain it is usually able to arrange meetings with leading businessmen and government officials – its strongest links being with the FCO and the Department of Trade. The list of British visitors helped by the Foundation is impressive. For instance, in 1978–9 MPs who visited the Republic included such prominent Conservatives as Douglas Hurd, Mark Carlisle and John Stanley.

Naturally most of the visits are for those who are likely to sympathize with the broad aims of the Foundation, but over the years a number of Labour politicians have also visited South Africa as its guests. John Mackintosh, the Labour MP, was one of these, and, indeed, wrote a very critical article in *The Times*, 'The Afrikaner Road to Disaster', when he returned. However, he was an exception. When Cecil Parkinson, Conservative minister of state at the Department of Trade, spoke in the Commons in May 1979, he referred to his visit to South Africa three years earlier, which had been sponsored by the Foundation. He argued, on the basis of what he had seen on that visit, that the expansion of the South African economy would have desirable social effects inside the country, especially for the black population. Furthermore, he stated that the British government's policy 'is that civil trade with other countries should be determined by commercial considerations, not by the character of the governments of those countries'. He emphasized the size and importance of Anglo/South African trade, and concluded: 'Our bilateral trade with South Africa is not peripheral to our economy. It is of central importance.'[28] The Foundation could have written the script.

UKSATA

The United Kingdom–South Africa Trade Association (UKSATA) was established in 1965 as a private limited company, with an initial membership of 55. By 1980, this had increased to about 300, and it still stands at just under this number. The members, who include many top names in British commerce and finance, are drawn together by their common economic interests in South Africa. UKSATA has a governing council from which an executive committee is drawn, but the bulk of the association's activities is undertaken by a small full-time staff under an executive director. The present director is Mr John McQuiggan, who previously served 24 years in the Foreign and Commonwealth Office, with wide African experience. The governing council is notable for the seniority of its members. The president is Lord Erroll of Hale, the vice-presidents are Lord Barber (the ex-Conservative chancellor) and Sir David

Scott (ex-ambassador to South Africa). The chairmanship, which rotates every three years, was held until 1982 by Mr G.A. Higham, chairman of Cape Industries.

UKSATA is careful to distinguish itself from the South Africa Foundation – not only in its British origins, but in its aims and activities. While the Foundation is concerned with building an image of South Africa which will preserve and reinforce Western contacts, UKSATA sees itself as an association whose exclusive concern is with trade and investment. One of its chief functions is to provide members with information about South African trading prospects, which is done in the director's monthly newsletter, or on individual request when members want specific information. The information is not necessarily confined to economic affairs, for it is recognized that political and social developments influence trade and investment. To provide this information, the staff calls on a range of sources – academic reports, the financial press, government reports, and so on – but occasionally it undertakes its own evaluations. In 1978, for instance, the director published a report on Britain's invisible earnings from South Africa, which he believed had been underestimated.[29] UKSATA literature, in general, emphasizes the size and importance of the economic relationship.

In facilitating trade between Britain and South Africa, the association has established a wide range of contacts in the governments and business communities of both countries. Within the British government its main links are with the FCO, the Department of Trade and Industry, the Treasury and the Bank of England. The government formally recognizes UKSATA as a channel of advice and expertise. In a somewhat mystic phrase, it is the 'chosen instrument' of the British Overseas Trade Board for expert advice on South Africa, and on the business side it is represented on the CBI's Overseas Directorate and a number of its sub-committees. Its contacts in South Africa are also good, and the chairman and executive director pay regular visits to the Republic to ensure the quality of their information. The 1982 Report reads: 'The Director made a five-week visit to South Africa in 1982 during which he had discussions with a number of South African Ministers and senior officials; Directors of the Reserve Bank and major international banks, leaders of South African industry and British subsidiary companies; Trade Union representatives; a number of Black leaders; Members of Parliament; some Homeland leaders; media representatives; and Directors of the main Trade, Commerce and Industry Associations.'[30] UKSATA also maintains strong ties with its sister organization in South Africa, the South Africa–Britain Trade Association (SABRITA), and the British Embassy gives help to visiting UKSATA officials.

Like the South African Foundation, UKSATA claims to be non-political. However, in earlier years, it was involved in considerable political controversy. The most striking case was in 1970 when the Zambian government accused Barclays Bank of activities prejudicial to the Zambian state. The basis of this was not the bank's operations in Zambia itself, but the fact that Sir Frederic Seebohm, the bank's chairman, served on the executive committee of UKSATA, which, said the Zambians, 'politically promoted the interests of South Africa in Britain'. Both the bank and UKSATA denied the accusations, but they were taken up by Charles Douglas-Home in *The Times*, who pointed to UKSATA's campaign against the arms ban on South Africa, and its criticism of Rhodesian sanctions. He asked whether Barclays, or any other business with interests in black Africa, could 'really afford to continue its membership of UKSATA if that membership threatens its business interests in the rest of Africa'.[31]

The accusations against UKSATA were based on the actions and statements of its leaders at the time. UKSATA's executive director, Mr George Mason, had publicly protested against Rhodesian sanctions, and the association had made no secret of its dislike of the arms ban. In June 1967 UKSATA's chairman, Mr W. E. Luke, told the membership: 'Your Executive Committee has been concerned with the effects of the arms embargo on our trade with South Africa, and it is hoped that there will be a possibility of some successful influence being exerted.'[32] In the following year he told the association that although the ban had not been lifted, 'the decision on the supply of arms was within an ace of being won and . . . the four Cabinet Ministers mainly concerned were, in fact, all on our side'.[33]

In more recent years the association has tried hard to lose its image as the right-wing friend of South Africa. It now refuses to involve itself in public discussions which it regards as 'political', and would, for example, refuse to join a broadcast debate with the AAM on apartheid. Under its new leadership, UKSATA has abandoned public stands on controversial issues, and it has shown a favourable response to the mildly reformist EEC Code of Conduct. It emphasizes that it receives no government funds, all its resources being raised by its members, and it is independent of all political parties (although, as is inevitable with a business organization, its strongest links are with the Conservatives). It continues, however, to be very conscious of the political pressures on it. It therefore refuses to publish lists of its members, and most of its services and publications are limited to the membership. It now works quietly and discreetly, and seldom reaches the public eye. UKSATA's non-political self-image is of course rejected by the AAM, for whom – like the Foundation – it is numbered among 'the collaborators'. The AAM would point to the association's own publication *What is UKSATA?* to underline its case, for there the objectives of UKSATA are said to include, one, acting on behalf of its members 'to maintain and strengthen trade with and to ensure the protection of their investments in South Africa', and, two, emphasizing to governments and other organizations the extent of the British stake in South Africa and the benefits that arise from that. In UKSATA eyes this is simply the promotion of trade without political implication, but the AAM sees it as direct support for apartheid.

UKSATA's broad views on the nature of the Anglo/South African relationship are to be found in the pamphlet *British Trade with South Africa*. This takes the view that, as a major trading nation, Britain had traditionally done business without regard to the internal policies of its trading partners, or even the current relations between the governments. It goes on to say: 'It is a simplistic and fallacious viewpoint that because companies trade with or invest in South Africa, they support apartheid.' Indeed, in the view of most UKSATA members, says the pamphlet, the reverse is the case: they believe that the lot of the blacks can best be improved by economic development, as many black leaders themselves believe. 'Thus an enormous investment in the human infrastructure of the country is necessary if the South African economy is to grow, and if black advancement is to develop.'[34]

Similar views were expressed at UKSATA's annual lunch in December 1979 by Mr Peter Blaker, the minister of state at the FCO in the new Thatcher administration. The lunch provides an opportunity for the government and business to exchange in public ideas on Anglo/South Africa relations. On this occasion the businessmen must have been reassured. Mr Blaker started by saying, as did Mrs Thatcher later in Washington, that the government's policy was 'to seek to reverse South Africa's isolation through working via our close bilateral contacts'. He welcomed the change in the international climate towards South Africa and spoke sympathetically of P. W. Botha's reforms. However, he emphasized that there was still a long way to go, and hoped that South Africa could move quickly enough 'to keep ahead of her critics and provide her friends with sufficient ammunition to hold off the baying demands being made in New York and elsewhere'. The government, he said, would continue to impose the arms ban, but was opposed to further sanctions; it was impossible to say that economic sanctions would 'never' be considered as a policy option, but the government did not believe that they would achieve their objectives. He concluded by emphasizing the excellent prospects for economic cooperation between the two countries.[35]

The British Council of Churches (BCC)
The churches recognize South Africa as one of their great moral issues – a Christian country which practises racial discrimination and claims to do so in defence of Western Christian civilization. The British Council of

Churches has wrestled regularly with the problems of the Republic. The day-to-day work on South Africa is handled by its International Division, which has given special attention to Africa, and has a separate Africa Secretary. Even if the BCC wanted to pay less attention to South Africa – and there is no evidence to suggest that it does – the Republic would continue to have a high priority because of the constant pressure from sister churches in Africa and the World Council of Churches (WCC). The International Division acts as a ginger group within the BCC, trying to ensure that attitudes in the British churches do not drift too far away from those in the world organization and other churches. The possibility of this happening was illustrated in 1971 when Archbishop Michael Ramsey presided over the meeting of the Anglican Consultative Council in Kenya – the first time that there were more African and Asian than white members. Ramsey, who was critical of the WCC's attitude to South Africa, started with a note of caution, saying that people who talk of fighting wars should be very clear about their objectives and the likely outcome, for they may not achieve the removal of oppression and injustice. His position, however, did not prevail; instead the council endorsed the WCC's 'Programme to Combat Racism'.

In Britain the BCC brings together the main Christian denominations (the Roman Catholic church sends observers), but in dealing with a controversial issue like South Africa it cannot dictate to the separate churches; rather, it provides a forum in which to search for some measure of agreement. This has not been easy in the case of South Africa, for there have been divisions both among the churches and among the individual Christians within them. The divisions have not been about apartheid, which is universally condemned as offensive to the teachings of Christ, but about the methods to be employed against it, with, for example, the Anglicans tending to be more cautious and conservative than the Methodists. The debates have focused on such questions as: Are double standards being used in judging South Africa? What methods are to be employed in encouraging reform in South Africa? What organizations should the churches support in promoting reform? Does the concern of church leaders – and particularly those most strongly committed on the South African issue – reflect the opinions of the congregations?

The different views within the churches over the methods to be employed against apartheid have emerged in debates on four major reports about South Africa which have been submitted to the BCC conferences – in 1965, 1970, 1973 and 1979. All these reports were the work of mixed groups of laymen and clerics. The 1965 report – *The Future of South Africa* – stated clearly that apartheid is a blasphemy against the Holy Spirit and it raised the spectre of race war, but the group showed no sympathy either for the use of force or even sanctions against South Africa. The general tone was one of reconciliation through discussion and prayer. 'Instinctively,' it said, 'we are against economic sanctions. We shrink from forcing our judgement on others, however much we may think the other person's views to be wrong.' Nor was it accepted that a race war had already started in South Africa and therefore violence should be met by violence. 'This is to accept the theory of the *jihad*, and to applaud the Crusades . . . the Christian witness is that violence can only beget violence, and that reconciliation cannot lie along that road.'[36]

The substance of the 1970 report – *Violence in Southern Africa - A Christian Assessment* – has already been outlined in Chapter 4. With its support for revolution and the use of violence against apartheid, it was entirely different from its predecessor in its assumptions and its values. When it was submitted to the BCC executive committee before the conference, the committee asked for some changes to be made, and when the group refused to do this, the committee decided that the report should be published separately later. In the event, it was reported at length in *The Observer*, and ended up by arousing strong reactions on all sides. This added fuel to the other issue which caused dispute at the 1970 conference: the WCC's 'special fund'. The WCC had proposed that funds should be made available not only to groups like the AAM but to black nationalist movements. According to the WCC, these grants were for 'humanitarian purposes', but the critics pointed to the nationalist movements' guerilla armies. British church leaders were publicly divided. The Archbishop of York (Dr Donald Coggan), emphasizing that the grants were for humanitarian work, supported the WCC, as did the President of the Methodists (The Revd Rupert Davies); whereas the Archbishop of Canterbury (Dr Michael Ramsey) regretted that the WCC council had not consulted the member churches and opposed the decision, and he was joined in this by the President of the Baptist Union (Sir Cyril Black).[37] In the final vote, despite many critical speeches, a clear majority endorsed the WCC action.

Shortly after this, the WCC pursued the issue of the special fund in its 'Programme to Combat Racism' (PCR). The programme specified that the fund's resources were 'to support organizations that combat racism rather than welfare organizations that alleviate the effect of racism'. It is within this spirit that funds have been given to black nationalist parties which are engaged in armed conflict, and although the WCC says that the funds are not for military uses, it also says that they are made 'without control of the manner in which they are spent, and are intended as an expression of commitment by the PCR to the cause of economic, social and political justice'.[38] (Controversy over the WCC's position continued, and, in the case of the Salvation Army, led first to the Army suspending its WCC membership in 1978, when support was given to the Patriotic Front fighting in Zimbabwe, and then, in 1981, withdrawing entirely.)

Perhaps because of the deep divisions created by the 1970 BCC report, when a new group was set up in 1972, it was to confine itself to looking at the question of investment. The report – *Investment in South Africa* – was published in 1973, and it had none of the fireworks of 1970. It was a cautious document in search of compromise. It did not accept the undiluted view that economic expansion in its own right promotes reform, but it did hope that change might be achieved through pressure on the part of British and other foreign companies operating in South Africa. It therefore recommended that a genuine effort should first be made at reform through contact, before any programme of dissociation was considered, and concluded with three recommendations: first, that the churches should promote a programme of study, information and education, both for the Christian community and for the general public; second, that companies should exercise pressure for reform, and contribute a proportion of their income to the advancement of black people; finally, if pressure for reform were unsuccessful, there should be economic withdrawal.[39] When the BCC conference debated the report, it showed the same spirit of moderation. It accepted that valuable changes in working conditions for blacks might be achieved through pressure, and gave support to the Codes of Conduct that had been designed to this end.

As for the 1979 BCC debate, it was based, like its predecessors, on a group report – *Political Change in South Africa: Britain's Responsibility*. The group argued that the constructive engagement approach of the 1973 report had failed and should be abandoned. It claimed that although some black working conditions had improved, 'the fundamental economic and political situation has remained the same, and the human predicament of many blacks has deteriorated'. The church could not stand aside from such 'gross institutionalized injustice'. It was therefore recommended that 'the churches should seek from the British government a commitment to support, or at least not to veto, proposals in the Security Council for sanctions against South Africa so long as the majority of the people are denied an effective voice in national decision-making'. In reaching its conclusions, the 1979 report marshalled a series of arguments against the 1973 position. It claimed that virtually no reference had been made to black views: 'The document was "our" assessment of what "we" should do,' whereas the liberation movements opposed foreign investment. Furthermore, research had been undertaken on the effect of the contact policy in South Africa which showed that the policy – including the EEC Code of Conduct – had failed to achieve the results claimed for it. Since constructive engagement had failed, it should be replaced by a policy of phased disengagement.[40]

When the report was debated in the BCC Assembly, there was the usual division of views, with some people querying whether the 'liberation movements' should be accepted as the legitimate voice of black South Africans, and therefore used as the basis for opposition to investment. In the vote, however, a strong majority supported the report, and the Assembly declared 'its conviction that progressive disengagement from the economy of South Africa is now the appropriate basic approach for the churches to adopt.' It was a dramatic reversal of the position of six years earlier, and the advice which emerged must have sounded extraordinary to those businessmen who studied it. Full disengagement was not to be implemented immediately – it was to be 'progressive' or 'phased' disengagement, with some flexibility retained. The mixed nature of the proposal was demonstrated by the suggestion that while economic relations were being phased out, the companies should continue to apply the EEC Code of Conduct, and temporary contact should be retained in such fields as academic and cultural activity. Firms should behave in such a way as to make easy their return to a reformed South Africa.

Two further issues were noted, but not clarified, in the 1979 report: the West's reliance on South African minerals, and the effect of the disengagement policy on the British economy. The report recognized that the effect of halting South African mineral supplies was difficult to assess, depending 'on the extent to which alternative supplies or substitutes can be developed', but did not pursue the matter further. As for the effect on the British economy, it said that the potential loss of business and investment elsewhere (e.g. Nigeria) must be taken into account. Meanwhile an assessment of the loss of jobs from a complete break with South Africa was said to be between 30,000 and 70,000, which was 'within the order of normal quarterly fluctuations in total employment. This represents a severe burden for those directly involved but one which is asked of many others as a result of policy choices in other fields.'

For the research about the impact of the contact policy, and the assessment of job losses, the 1979 report relied heavily upon work undertaken by Christian Concern for Southern Africa (CCSA) – a small Christian group established for study and research. Among its activities CCSA has arranged conferences, written and commissioned reports, and combined with other groups in study of such matters as black trade unions, British investments, and the operations of British companies and banks. Some of this work has had a considerable impact. For instance, ICI was so concerned at a CCSA report on the company's policies in South Africa – in which CCSA suggested a shift from rapid commercial expansion to greater support for the black community – that it arranged for senior executives to visit CCSA. However, CCSA has not escaped the tensions which have characterized the churches' response to southern Africa. By 1977, severe internal division had developed about its role: should it retain its original task of research and information, or should it become more radical and more directly involved? By 1978, the radical view had become predominant, with the report for that year openly rejecting the policy of constructive engagement (although it was then still BCC policy), and, of its own position, saying that 'CCSA either should be replaced by a campaigning body or should have its terms of reference widened, so that it can operate on a broader front'.[41] The radical tone persisted in the evidence given to the 1979 BCC working group and in subsequent publications.

Although there has been division within the British churches over the way to oppose apartheid, there has been enough common ground for the BCC and the separate denominations to launch campaigns against South Africa's racial policies. Four broad strategies have been employed: pressure on the government, pressure on business and financial organizations, alerting church members and awakening the Christian conscience, and contributing towards the broad social climate of criticism of apartheid. Within those strategies a variety of tactics have been employed, reflecting different attitudes within the churches. Some Christian leaders have led anti-apartheid rallies in Trafalgar Square; others have tried to build stronger links with churches in the Republic; others have sought to influence government and business leaders in Britain and South Africa through personal contacts; some have joined in national media debates; others have attended conferences about apartheid; and many have spoken to their congregations about South Africa.

A regular feature of the attempts to influence government have been delegations to ministers led by eminent churchmen. Sometimes they have gone to express general concern, but on other occasions they have made very specific proposals. Thus the 1979 BCC conference set out in detail the steps that it thought government and business organizations should take, calling on the government to recognize South Africa as a threat to world peace; to extend the arms embargo to cover all technology that might be valuable to armed forces; to remove trade credits; and to withdraw the commercial staff from the British Embassy.[42] In much broader terms, the churches have also sought to create a moral climate in which decisions in government and business are taken. As the 1965 report said, 'Christians will expect the government to take account of the deep moral issues involved.' It accused the government of 'conniving with' apartheid because it was then selling arms and granting South Africa the equivalent of Commonwealth preferences.

In building up this moral climate, the BCC has seen southern Africa in a world-wide Christian context – stressing the importance of black Africa in the extension of the faith, the danger of the British churches failing to bear witness on a universal moral issue, and the need to retain harmony with

Christians elsewhere. A different international question is the attitude to be adopted towards the churches in South Africa, both black and white. There have been strong ties between British and South African churches since the early missionary days, and this continues in the English-speaking churches through conferences, and through clergy moving between the two countries. The problems which tax the British churches are whether those contacts should be retained, and if so on what terms.

Finally, the churches have been eager to influence public opinion. The 1970 BCC report spoke of the need for a propaganda campaign against South Africa. That of 1973 called for 'a programme of study, information and education, both of the Christian community and the general public'. The 1979 report recommended that the churches address themselves 'primarily to the government and the electorate at large'. As with the AAM and the black states, the churches' stand against apartheid has contributed primarily to the steady movement of opinion against racial discrimination, rather than having any sharp impact. For those who deal in eternity, the time-scale may seem less frustrating than it has for the AAM.

South Africa's secret services
As a postscript to this chapter, a word needs to be said about South Africa's secret services. The South Africans are clearly aware of the importance of the British groups, and have directed their secret services against them. (The name of these services has changed from time to time, but for convenience the familiar BOSS – the Bureau of State Security – will be used here.) Obviously, information is difficult to obtain and must often be speculative, but it would appear that BOSS has been active in Britain and has directed its activities not only against the pressure groups, but against the exiled South African parties, and perhaps even against the British Labour and Liberal parties.

As far as the pressure groups are concerned, there have been reports of BOSS activities against both the AAM and certain Christian anti-apartheid groups. One of the Christian groups involved is the Defence and Aid Fund (D and AF), which was formed in 1956 under the auspices of Christian Action and the leadership of Canon Collins of St Martin-in-the-Fields.[43] Its aims are to help defend those accused of 'political' crimes in South Africa, to relieve the distress of their dependants and to work for a non-racial society. According to a 1981 *Sunday Times* 'Insight' report, a South African agent, Jean Legrange, started to do some voluntary work for Christian Action in 1968, and shortly afterwards managed to get a job in the D and AF office.[44] There is dispute about how much damage she was able to do there, for Canon Collins said that she had no access to confidential files, whereas there are other claims that she obtained information and helped to arrange a burglary of confidential files which subsequently led to arrests in South Africa.

The AAM, too, has also been concerned about penetration by South African agents. In 1971 Mrs Ethel de Keyser, the AAM secretary, told a court that she believed that South African police spies attended AAM meetings. To reinforce this claim, there have been confessions from men like Gordon Winter,[45] a British journalist who had been working in South Africa, and Ivan Himmelhoch,[46] a South African law student, that they spied on the AAM for BOSS, and from Charles Richardson, a London gang leader, that he burgled the AAM offices for the South Africans. There have been similar reports of burglaries and penetration by spies of the exiled South African parties. According to Gordon Winter, one of the most successful penetrations was in the 1960s by Hans Lombard, a South African journalist. According to Winter, Lombard not only established a friendship with Fenner Brockway, the Labour MP, which opened doors into the anti-apartheid groups, but penetrated the Pan-African Congress (PAC). Winter says that Lombard obtained a list of about 4,000 PAC members which was later used by the South African government in a wave of arrests which broke the back of the party in the Republic.

The South Africans may also have directed secret service activities against the Labour and Liberal parties because of their stand against apartheid. No less a figure than Sir Harold Wilson believed this. In 1976, near the end of his premiership, he told the Commons that South African organizations were framing British political figures, including the leader of the Liberal Party, Jeremy Thorpe.[47] In Thorpe's case, Wilson turned out to be wrong, but some of his other suspicions have been less easy to explain away and his claim that the South Africans had tried to discredit certain British politicians was fully supported by Gordon Winter.

There is no certain evidence to confirm these accusations, but among the alleged attempts to discredit individuals the case of Peter Hain has never been satisfactorily explained. Hain was charged but acquitted of robbing a bank in 1975. Hain believes that the situation was set up by the South Africans, and Winter supports this view, saying that BOSS employed a young criminal who was Hain's double to commit the offence. The broader implication of trying to tilt the balance of British politics towards the Conservatives may have been based on a South African calculation that a significant change was taking place in British politics during the early 1970s. The two main parties had roughly equal but declining support, whereas the Liberals were gaining in strength. Therefore, so the calculation may have gone, even a small shift in voting patterns could alter the balance. In such a situation, it was in South Africa's interests to discredit the Liberal Party because it was such a vociferous opponent of apartheid in its own right, and also because it was drawing votes away from the Conservatives to the advantage of the Labour Party. If that was the intention, it was unsuccessful. The main South African effort appears to have been made before the elections of 1974, but in these two elections the Labour Party regained office at the expense of the Conservatives, while the Liberals enjoyed a revival.

When mention is made of 'decision-makers', it is often taken to mean decision-makers in government. In Britain's relations with South Africa, an equally important part is played by decision-makers outside the government. Moreover, the government has neither the desire nor the ability (short of emergency conditions) to impose its control over the full range of the contacts. Thus a striking characteristic of the Anglo/South African relationship is not only the plurality of the contacts but the plurality of the British decision-makers. By way of illustration, one may cite a few of the organizations which have imposed some form of sanctions against the Republic. The list includes the British Actors Equity Association, which has banned its members from visits; the Longbenton Council, which was the first of several local authorities to ban the purchase of South African goods; the Methodist Church, which has sold its shares in RTZ and Hill Samuel; and the Department of Trade, which issued the government order banning the sale of arms.[1]

While many organizations would prefer to restrict themselves to their own specialist fields, they are seldom able to do so because the anti-apartheid groups insist on introducing broader issues. This has happened in sport, much to the consternation of the British sporting bodies. For example, in 1981 when a proposal was made that South Africa should be readmitted to test cricket because of improved racial integration in that sport, Archbishop Trevor Huddleston, president of the AAM, wrote to *The Times* saying that the South Africans 'must show the world that apartheid itself has been totally abolished in every sphere of life. As a start they can abolish the pass laws; they can release Nelson Mandela and all other political prisoners; they can provide homes and jobs in the Western Cape for the dispossessed people of Nyanga, and they can stop trying to deceive the world by claiming that their racist ideology is a bulwark against communism. Until such actions are taken South Africa must expect sport to be used as a political weapon.'[2]

Thus the debate is extended outside the particular sport, in this case cricket, to cover such questions as whether race relations in South Africa will be improved by contact or by isolation; whether progress in one field should be rewarded, or whether more will be achieved by intensifying pressure in other areas of the apartheid system where no progress has been made; and what the effect will be on other international contacts. In 1981, the choice for the English cricket authorities boiled down to whether they accepted the views of the West Indies, Pakistan and India that South Africa should be excluded, or whether they split international cricket apart.

In their day-to-day activities, however, decision-makers are usually dealing with their own kind – churchmen with churchmen, government officials with government officials, and sport administrators with sport administrators – and within each group norms and priorities are established. Thus, among businessmen, there is a strong consensus that economic links with South Africa are beneficial to all. One of the consequences of such group consensus is bewilderment and resentment when outside pressures – usually interpreted as outside 'interference' – are applied. The mutual incomprehension which results was apparent in 1970 when Peter Hain, again in the context of the cricket establishment, said that he was faced by 'people concerned with cricket to the exclusion of all else'. He concluded that 'it was impossible to *communicate* with them, let alone reason with them'.[3] Doubtless the cricket authorities concluded that it was impossible to communicate with people like Hain because they can think of nothing but opposition to apartheid.

Yet there is no escape from the outside pressures. This was recognized in a report by the Business International Corporation of New York on the position of multinationals in the Republic during the 1980s. It predicted that in the West pressure would continue to increase from the anti-apartheid groups, while inside South Africa neither the government nor the black nationalists would be able to force a decisive conclusion. Although the government was strong enough to prevent a successful revolution, it would not be able to avoid increased racial clashes. Companies were advised to accept the growing importance of trade unions, even though, in the absence of alternative outlets, they were likely to be used for political ends.[4] Such advice points up a common complaint of businessmen: that in South Africa they have to base their decisions not on commercial prospects but on political considerations which are out of their hands.

To turn now to decision-making within government, policy, according to one definition, 'evolves in a continuing dialogue between the responsible ministers and their civil servants, a continuing interaction between political direction and the pressures of established practice and administrative interests'. It builds up incrementally – 'an accumulation of small decisions, of adjustments to circumstances and reactions to situations'.[5] The British tend to treat each issue that arises over South Africa as a discrete problem – whether it be incursions into Angola,

Namibia, sports boycotts or arms bans – whereas the black states and the anti-apartheid groups characteristically urge a comprehensive stand against apartheid. As a result, the British often find themselves responding to the initiative of others, rather than initiating policy themselves. There are exceptions to this, such as the role that they played in promoting the EEC Code of Conduct and the Contact Group for Namibia, but even these cases may be seen as attempts to counter anticipated pressure.

The incremental style of decision-making prospers within a broad political consensus, and one of the features of British South African policy has been its relative consistency over the years. Indeed a frequent complaint of the AAM to Labour governments has been that their South African policies are indistinguishable from those of the Tories. Yet changes have taken place, with differences of emphasis, if not of direction, between the ruling parties. This was illustrated in the dispute over the sale of arms in 1970, and emerged again in parliamentary debates which fell either side of the Conservative election victory of 1979. In December 1978, a few months before the election, Malcolm Rifkind, then a Conservative backbencher, introduced a debate on sanctions against South Africa. He said that all previous governments, Labour and Conservative alike, had taken a common stand against sanctions, but that there were signs of the present Labour administration abandoning this. He noted that firms had been asked to estimate the effect that sanctions would have on them, and that the British government had abstained on a Security Council resolution warning South Africa that sanctions might follow a failure to reach a solution on Namibia.[6] In reply, Mr Ted Rowlands, the minister of state at the Foreign Office, said that British policy was to try to avoid sanctions, but it was impossible to rule them out entirely. However, the government was certainly not thrusting forward thoughtlessly, for it realized that cutting economic links with South Africa could have 'severe repercussions on the domestic economy'.[7]

The background to the Labour government's reassessment of Britain's position was both its concern at the long-term implications of economic dependence on South Africa, and its response to the immediate pressures on the Republic following the Soweto riots and the death of Steve Biko. The change can be traced during the 1970s. In 1974, James Callaghan (then foreign secretary) had confirmed, like ministers in previous govern-ments, that 'so far as normal trade and investment are concerned, firms remain free to carry out existing or future contracts with South Africa', and he said that the usual range of government services would be available because the government did not believe that the political complexion of a foreign government should interfere in these matters.[8] However, by late 1977 the government's position had changed. In November 1977, Denis Healey, the chancellor of the exchequer, told the Commons that the government would discourage new investment in South Africa, and Alex Lyon, the Labour backbencher, claimed that the cabinet had gone further by deciding to support disinvestment.[9] The 1978 'Rifkind debate' confirmed the change of attitude.

Whether, once the riots and the deaths had slipped from the headlines, the Labour government would have implemented changes must be an open question; what is clear is that when Margaret Thatcher's government came to power in May 1979, all such thoughts disappeared. The new government quickly confirmed that it had no intention of reducing economic links. As we have noted, Cecil Parkinson, the minister of state at the Department of Trade, speaking in a Commons debate in May 1979, made a special point that 'civil trade with other countries should be determined by commercial considerations, not by the character of the governments of those countries', and underlined the particular importance of South African trade. This view was taken a step further by Mrs Thatcher herself, who told the Foreign Policy Association in the USA that 'there is now a real prospect that the conflicts on South Africa's borders, in Rhodesia and Namibia, will shortly be ended. This, combined with the welcome initiatives in South Africa's domestic policies, offers a chance to defuse the crisis which was potentially of the utmost gravity, and to make progress towards an early ending of the isolation of South Africa in world affairs.'[10] Mrs Thatcher's critics might argue that the speech showed her failure to appreciate the international opposition to South Africa and the limited options open to Britain, but it certainly signalled a shift in the British government's position. Constructive contact and dialogue were now the watchwords, not isolation and ostracism.[11]

The implications, however, of this shift in attitudes should not be exaggerated. This has become clear as the constraints of office have closed in on the Conservatives. For example, the Thatcher government has been less enthusiastic than its Labour predecessor over the EEC Code of Conduct. It has been reluctant to publish the names of firms that have failed to comply, and civil servants, absorbing the flavour of the new administration, have been less energetic in administering it. But there has been no thought of abandoning it, for that would have created a furore among Britain's European partners and a row at home, nor could the government entirely turn a blind eye to breaches of the code, which still attract some media and parliamentary attention. Similarly, with other policy issues, the constraints are clear. There is no chance of the Thatcher government lifting the arms ban, as the Heath government had done less than ten years before, for the ban is now backed by a UN mandatory resolution; nor of recognizing the 'independence' claimed by the South African government for the black homelands; and, although the talk of sanctions is now muffled, the search for an internationally acceptable Namibian solution continues.

Similarly, although the degree of personal commitment to South Africa varies among ministers, none has been able to avoid involvement. Some, like David Owen, Alec Douglas-Home and (if Rhodesia is included) Harold Wilson, have been deeply committed. In the early days of the Rhodesian crisis the search for a solution became almost an obsession with Wilson – 'his Cuba', as he called it.[12] David Owen's commitment to southern Africa during his foreign secretaryship led to a period when, exceptionally, Britain took initiatives rather than waiting on events – with involvement in the Anglo-American proposals for Rhodesia, the intro-duction of the EEC Code of Conduct, the formation of the Contact Group on Namibia, and government support for the UN Anti-Apartheid Year. Yet, for all his efforts, Owen could not throw off the constraints which surround British policy. The Rhodesian proposals ran into the sands of disagreement between Smith and the Patriotic Front, the Contact Group failed to make quick progress, the EEC Code of Conduct was only partially successful, and Owen's very commitment limited his influence with the South African government, for he was accused of prejudice against the whites, as well as of personal arrogance. Other prime ministers and foreign secretaries have shown less enthusiasm for southern African affairs. Edward Heath, although he was deeply embroiled in the arms sales dispute, gave the impression when in office that southern African affairs were forced upon him. Lord Carrington, despite achieving the Rhodesian settlement, a prize that had eluded all the efforts of Wilson, Home and Owen, did not give southern Africa a top priority. The story goes that when another southern African problem was put on his desk shortly after the Rhodesian settlement, he remarked that he had hoped not to hear much of that part of the world for a year or two.

Less dramatic than the personal commitment of political leaders, but at least as important, is the role of the departments of government. The balance of importance has changed as the nature of Britain's involvement has changed. In the past, the ministry of defence and the services were prominent because of the defence alliance. That has gone, and the economic side of the relationship now predominates. The result is that the departments with responsibility for trade and financial matters play major roles. The emphasis of the Foreign Office's work has also changed. Sir David Scott, on taking up his post as British ambassador in 1976, noted that 'although Britain still had close and valuable connections with the Republic in the economic and commercial fields, the Ambassador could no longer expect to be closely involved in the political scene', and that on the political front both sides 'tended to keep their distance'.[13] In fact, the situation turned out to be less clear-cut than this, and Sir David later found himself enmeshed in the 'political' negotiations over Rhodesia and Namibia, and found that international hostility to the Republic intruded into all his work.

Policy coordination is well developed in the British government, and through the decision-making process an 'official view' usually emerges which is broadly shared by all departments. There are fewer of the overt bureaucratic struggles that characterize the US government, but nevertheless differences do arise within and between departments, and especially on an issue like relations with South Africa in which so many interests and values are involved and on which the government is subjected to persistent pressures. There have even been differences within the Foreign Office. The memory is still clear of Lord Caradon's visits to Whitehall during his period as British representative at the United Nations. He would return full of enthusiasm from New York to urge greater efforts against South Africa and Rhodesia only to find that his sense of urgency was not always matched in London and even less in the British Embassy in Pretoria. Between the departments there is constant bargaining and jockeying for position so that the 'official view' is usually a compromise of departmental positions.

Insight into the attitudes and workings of the departments as regards South Africa is provided by two investigations. The first, mentioned in Chapter 4, was that undertaken by the Trade and Industry Sub-Committee of the Expenditure Committee in 1973–4 to investigate the conditions of black employees working for British firms in South Africa.[14] Most of the evidence was taken from private companies, but one session was given over to departmental officials. They were led by Sir Max Brown, from the Department of Trade and Industry, who had with him two members of his own department and one each from the Foreign Office and the Treasury. Before the meeting, the Department of Trade and Industry had submitted a memorandum outlining the support it gave to British trade and investment in South Africa. This showed that the Republic was treated as any other country with good economic prospects, so that 'in line with practice ... export opportunities in South Africa are brought to the attention of United Kingdom firms'. For those firms considering establishing a subsidiary in the Republic, some advice was available on black wages and conditions of employment. The memo went on to stress the importance of British investments in the Republic, and added that the resources which the department committed to promoting economic contacts with South Africa were smaller than the trade and investment figures warranted.

When the MPs came to question the officials, a gulf of attitudes opened up. The MPs made plain that the officials, and especially those in the Department of Trade and Industry, had been far too complacent about working conditions for blacks. William Rodgers complained of the department's 'very muted voice', and Mark Hughes referred to the guidance given to firms as 'milk-and-water stuff', telling them the least they could get away with. When the Foreign Office representative was questioned, he spoke of the government's interest in 'peaceful evolution and not violent change', and he recognized that the behaviour of British firms could play a part in this. His emphasis was therefore different from that of the trade officials, and he was treated more leniently by the MPs. Nevertheless he expressed strong reservations about attempts to monitor or control British firms abroad. He said: 'If it appeared that the Foreign Office, through legislative provision or otherwise, was acting as a sort of policeman, supervising the activities of British firms abroad, I would think this could have undesirable consequences and implications.' Sir Max Brown quickly endorsed this, and later added: 'I doubt very much whether one could think of enforcing anything in South Africa by any action taken in this country.' Despite these protests, the sub-committee report concluded that the advice given to firms by the Department of Trade and Industry was 'totally inadequate', and recommended a much more vigorous approach for the future, including the introduction of a code of practice.[15]

The second investigation – that of the Bingham Commission, which reported in 1978 – concerned the breaking of sanctions against Rhodesia by transporting oil through South Africa.[16] The departments had been divided about sanctions even before UDI. Sir Arthur Snelling, who had responsibility for the policy at the Commonwealth Office, later reflected on the attitudes of different departments. 'The Board of Trade,' he said, 'hated the idea of economic sanctions because it would get in the way of certain of their departmental objectives ... The Treasury didn't want us to block Rhodesia's sterling balances in the event of UDI for fear that other governments would fear that action of a similar sort would be taken against them, thus weakening confidence in sterling.'[17]

The Bingham Commission's report revealed the strong relationship that can develop between a government department and its 'constituency' (the groups and organizations with whom it regularly works). In this case, it was between the Ministry of Power (later the Department of Energy) and the oil companies. The ministry officials shared the companies' view that oil sanctions were neither practical nor desirable. In the early days of sanctions, the Foreign Office, conscious of the international pressures on Britain, called for greater efforts to stop the flow of oil, but it met with resistance both from the Ministry of Power and from the oil companies. Notes taken by an oil company representative at a meeting between the department and the companies in January 1967 reveal the pattern of the relationship: 'Whenever the Foreign Office raises the subject of "limiting" supplies to either Mozambique or South Africa, the Ministry of Power has always advised them that limitation of such supplies was not practical, nor would it be effective, and that furthermore it could not be expected that British oil companies would participate in any such schemes on a voluntary basis.'[18] It was agreed to call a further meeting, this time involving the Foreign Office, and that, in order 'to make the standpoint of the companies quite clear to the Foreign Office', officials from the Ministry of Power would attend, so that they could 'add their views to ours'. In the end it was the views of the oil companies and the Ministry of Power that prevailed; a blind eye was turned to the breaking of oil sanctions.

Policy objectives and options

There is a temptation to seek a single overriding objective in the British government's policy towards South Africa. Geoffrey Berridge, in his study of Anglo/South African relations, argues that Britain's need to retain economic links has been predominant and has created a situation which the South African government has been able to exploit.[19] Berridge recognizes that this may appear odd in a relationship in which Britain has much the larger economy, and he explains the discrepancy in terms of a British trade dependence on South Africa, which, although an apparently insignificant proportion of total trade, has contained 'items which are of enormous consequence to British industry, its energy and defence policies, and for the Bank of England's financial role'. The overall result has 'amounted to a formidable economic grip on Britain',[20] a situation which the South African government has exploited with toughness and skill in its diplomacy.

Without doubt the retention of economic links has been a high priority for Britain, and the South Africans have taken advantage of the situation in their diplomacy. Support for Berridge's position comes in the persistent protests of British governments (both Labour and Conservative) that Britain cannot afford an economic war with South Africa. Yet, this said, Berridge's argument does not take sufficient account of the many other factors involved. One of his examples to illustrate South Africa's use of economic power demonstrates this very point. He says that in their attempts to persuade the British government to lift the arms ban in 1967, the South Africans used both the gold and the trade 'weapons'. While the Labour government was debating the issue, the South Africans offered to channel all their gold through London, an action which they backed by the threat (later implemented) that if the ban were reaffirmed, they would go elsewhere for their imports. Despite this, the arms ban was retained.

There are several accounts of this decision from British ministers who were directly involved, and although they differ in emphasis, they are consistent in their recognition of the complexity of the situation and the number of factors that had to be balanced. The importance of the economic considerations was certainly understood, for the whole question of whether or not to resume arms sales had arisen because Britain was again facing an economic crisis. George Brown, the foreign secretary, favoured the sales, underlining the advantages for the British arms industry and the danger of South African retaliation against other British goods, as well as the need to protect British strategic interests.[21] Richard Crossman recorded in his diary that the Foreign Office, the Ministry of Defence and the Commonwealth Office combined to make a 'formidable line-up' in favour of the sales. Yet the decision went against them, because other departments and ministers had different priorities.[22] These included Harold Wilson, the prime minister. Wilson's attitude seems to have been a compound of personal commitment against the sale, fear of a split in the Labour Party and an appreciation of the international opposition that would arise. He says in his memoirs that he told the cabinet that if the arms sales were to be decided on economic criteria alone, 'regardless of wider overseas policy issues, regardless of moral issues', then the same should apply to all policy, including relations with Eastern Europe.[23]

The search for a single overriding objective in Britain's relations with South Africa is a false one. As this study has sought to show, there is a multiplicity of organizations and groups that help to shape the British side of the relationship. As for the government, it seeks to balance a number of aims: the pursuit of Britain's economic and strategic interests, the protection of its own position both at home and abroad, and the encouragement of some kind of reform in the Republic. In May 1981 the Commons Foreign Affairs Committee stated that 'the United Kingdom has a very real interest in encouraging peaceful change in South Africa both for its own sake and to safeguard British and wider Western interests there.' Yet no government has attempted to outline a precise programme of reform. That is partly in deference to South Africa's sovereignty, and partly a recognition of the clash of opinions at home. But there is also a prime need to retain a flexible position in a situation in which black expectations and white responses, both in South Africa and internationally, are constantly changing. Thus Mrs Thatcher's administration shifted its position away from support of the Smith/Muzorewa government, not from a change of heart about Rhodesia, but with an eye on its international position. If the British had gone ahead in recognizing the regime, it would certainly have had an adverse effect on their status abroad.

Concern with international status is particularly marked in such a politicized issue as relations with South Africa. This leads to symbolic policies, which all governments practise, not least the black states. A British example is found in the evidence that George Thomson gave to the Bingham Commission. Thomson admitted that by 1968 the government knew that Rhodesia was receiving a steady supply of oil, but, although it had given up hope of stopping this, he thought it important that British firms had no direct hand in it. He rejected the criticism that the policy was 'cosmetic'. 'It did matter', he told Bingham, 'that Britain should be seen not to be knowingly leaking oil into Rhodesia ... Nor would I accept the term "cosmetic" in terms of the political realities of the time. I understand what is meant by it perfectly well, but a great deal of politics itself is normally a problem of presentation.' Thomson concluded: 'If we had been shown to be careless about this matter, just acquiescing in the oil companies going on with the position where it could be said that knowingly British companies were allowing oil to go to Rhodesia, then that would have done us immense harm at the UN and elsewhere.'[24]

When one looks to the future, there are five basic approaches that will influence British decision-making: cooperation, constructive engagement, disengagement, pressure for reform, and confrontation. Supporters of the first, 'cooperation', reject South Africa's pariah status; they believe in 'normal relations', and emphasize the benefits that Britain gains from the South African connection. They give relatively little attention to the hostile international environment, or the racial problems inside the Republic, arguing that these should be settled by the South Africans themselves. Advocates of this approach are most commonly found among right-wing Conservatives, in business and financial circles, and in the departments of government associated with economic activities.

While one side of the cooperative approach urges that the South Africans should be left alone to sort out their problems, there is another, more positive, side which argues strongly in favour of economic co-operation as a way to break down apartheid. According to this argument, sometimes known as the Oppenheimer thesis (after the former chairman of the Anglo-American Corporation), apartheid survives because of slow economic growth.[25] Lack of investment and the absence of economic activity curtail the number of jobs available in the advanced sector of the economy, which means that there are enough whites to fill the skilled jobs. If South Africa could achieve a growth rate in excess of 5 per cent, blacks would be drawn into skilled jobs, their income would increase, and from their economic power political power would follow. Economic expansion therefore benefits all, and especially the blacks. Since there is no way of proving or disproving this argument, British businessmen and financiers, armed with the seductive thesis that morality and profit go hand in hand, are unlikely to abandon it.

The cooperative approach finds supporters also among military leaders and sports organizers, but their position is more difficult. As far as some military leaders and members of the Conservative Party are concerned, the advantages of military cooperation – South Africa's reliability against communist expansion, and the need to secure the Cape route and mineral supplies – more than outweigh the hostility of the black states and the anti-apartheid groups. Military cooperation, however, rests on a clear-cut government decision to work directly with the Republic, and successive British governments, from conviction and/or recognition of the adverse international reaction, have opposed that. The situation for sports organizers is less straightforward. The government does not exercise direct control (although it has been drawn in, as witnessed by the Gleneagles Agreement), and where the black states have had little say in the sport, as in rugby, tennis or golf, the sports authorities have usually favoured cooperation; but when the blacks have been able to threaten the sport, as is the case with cricket, they have reluctantly decided against co-operation. Yet even in a sport like rugby the diversity of British views emerges, with J.V. Smith, president of the Rugby Football Union in 1982, questioning the continuation of links with South Africa.

The second approach, 'constructive engagement' (or 'constructive contact', as it is sometimes called), rests on the view that satisfactory reform can be achieved through dialogue and contact. Unlike the advocates of cooperation, who tend to ignore the internal problems, or to assume that they will be solved by economic development, the supporters of constructive engagement recognize that there must be reform, for the sake of the whites as well as the blacks. They believe that white South Africans are open to influence, and that change is more likely to be achieved by 'positive' rather than 'negative' sanctions (i.e. rewards for progress rather than punishments for failure).

Constructive engagement was the approach favoured by Mrs Thatcher in her 1979 speech to the US Foreign Policy Association, and it accurately reflects the attitude of her government. Its most vocal advocates, however, have been the members of the Reagan administration. As noted in Chapter 2, it has been the line adopted by Chester Crocker, the Assistant Secretary of State for African Affairs, who in August 1981 described the USA as seeking 'to build a more constructive relationship with South Africa, one based on shared interests, persuasion and improved communication.'[26] When a US official was asked how America could defend its refusal to condemn the South African invasion of Angola, he replied: 'We have established a fragile dialogue with South Africa and it is essential that at least one Western country is prepared to discuss the problems with even-handedness. We're in touch with all participants including the Front Line states and SWAPO, and we therefore have a general sense of what can fly with all parties.'[27]

When one turns to 'disengagement', the third approach, the common intention is clear – to keep South Africa at a distance – but the motives behind this vary, as does the degree of disengagement proposed. One motive is moral indignation: a determination not to be associated with the evil of apartheid. Much of the discussion at the British Council of Churches and the Labour Party conferences falls into this category. A more hard-headed motive, which has already been discussed, is concern at Britain's economic reliance on South Africa, for, in David Owen's words, 'we stand to lose more than most if things go wrong.'[28] Another such hard-headed reason is the attempt to avoid international criticism and hostility. The argument here could be summarized as follows: 'Little but problems and difficulties lie ahead in South Africa. Continued racial clashes are inevitable, but the outcome is uncertain and the time-scale of any changes, whatever they may be, is impossible to predict. Britain's chances of influencing those changes are small, and therefore we pay the heavy price of international criticism, potential division at home and rebuffs in South Africa, all for little purpose. Britain's best option is to keep its head beneath the barricades, accept what economic advantages can be achieved without arousing too much criticism, but try to lower contact with the Republic and probably with the region as a whole.' The advantage of this approach is that it leaves responsibility for contacts with South Africa to non-governmental bodies, and thus might enable the government to avoid much of the criticism that comes from close association with the Republic.

The fourth approach, 'pressure for reform', shares with 'constructive engagement' the view that Britain should use its links with South Africa to promote reform, but differs over the methods to be employed and the extent of the reforms to be promoted. In this case, 'negative' as well as 'positive' sanctions are envisaged, because it is assumed that the South Africans will not introduce adequate reform unless they are forced into it. The aim is to use existing links to exert that pressure. The EEC Code of Conduct is an example of this policy – albeit a mild one. The code, which applies to Community firms operating in the Republic, was agreed at the Council of Ministers in September 1977 in order to forestall criticism of the EC's economic link with South Africa at the first UN Anti-Apartheid Conference, which was about to be held in Lagos. From the beginning, therefore, the code was designed to defend the European governments from international criticism, as well as to stimulate reform in South Africa. From the British government's point of view, it has the advantage of spreading the load of responsibility – not only internationally but at home. For the implementation of the code – as regards rates of pay, working conditions, union rights – is not by government but by business companies. Since the code is voluntary, the government can do no more than urge the companies to comply.

It could be argued that this is an ideal democratic situation, for the government, having demonstrated its concern by introducing the code, can then adopt a reactive pose and await public opinion – which in fact means the amount of attention generated by MPs, pressure groups and the mass media. It can then give the code greater or less attention depending on that response. There are, however, tensions in the situation. Some companies complain that they are being asked to do the government's dirty work, others believe that the code is unrealistic in South African conditions; some firms have failed to make reports, others make inadequate reports, and even those firms which comply do so in narrow terms, confining themselves to specific working conditions and terms of employment. Most firms, however, at least accept the code – which is more than many anti-apartheid groups do. They believe it ignores the fundamental problems of South African society. 'The system of apartheid', one critic writes, 'is not simply a set of rather dubious labour practices within employing establishments. It is a state-instituted system which provides the essential context in which everyone is compelled to live, and within which any investing company, however pure its own employment practices, chooses to operate... There is no way in which foreign direct investment in South Africa can avoid serving as a prop to the system of apartheid.'[29]

The Code of Conduct is a mild example of 'pressure for reform'; tougher measures are practised through limited, selective sanctions, such as the arms ban and sports boycotts. However, even with these measures the assumption remains that there is a chance to break apartheid through peaceful pressure. Advocates of 'confrontation', the last approach, do not accept that. They would prefer to see the British government support the black nationalists, and their guerrilla fighters; but since there is no chance of this, they press for economic sanctions. To this extent, there is some common ground between 'pressure for reform' and 'confrontation', but there are critical differences. First, the advocates of the former favour selective sanctions, whereas the supporters of 'confrontation' call for mandatory, comprehensive sanctions. Second, for those who favour 'confrontation' the sanctions are an adjunct to the armed liberation struggle, for they believe that only through force will apartheid be defeated. Abdul Minty, of the AAM, argues that the effectiveness of the armed struggle in Angola, Mozambique and Zimbabwe has assured a successful outcome to the revolution in South Africa, but economic sanctions would speed the process, reduce the bloodshed and demonstrate Western support for the black nationalists.[30]

The pros and cons of imposing economic sanctions, particularly mandatory comprehensive sanctions, have produced some of the fiercest debates about Britain's relations with South Africa. Those in favour naturally see the fewest problems in implementing them. According to D. G. Clarke, writing in 1980, the legal obstacles for UN members have been cleared away, the moral issues are now more widely accepted, and 'the technical capability and knowledge about how to enforce economic sanctions and manage the attendant adjustment problems has itself increased considerably.'[31] The supporters of comprehensive sanctions are, however, in a frustrating position, for the imposition of sanctions depends upon a government which has shown no enthusiasm for them, and, if ever they were imposed, their implementation would rest with those who are the most sceptical about their desirability and effectiveness – the business community and the officials in the trade and finance departments. This scepticism was partly formed and partly reinforced by the sanctions against Rhodesia, which, it is claimed, showed that such measures do not achieve their political aims, cause divisions at home, are impossible to implement effectively, and create strains among allies. A further major argument against sanctions is that it would be impossible to impose them against South Africa without seriously hurting neighbouring black states. It is argued that the impact would be much greater on some of these states than on South Africa itself, for their economic dependence would enable the South Africans to make sure that the black states suffered.[32]

The cautious, hesitant policies of the British government towards South Africa have drawn persistent criticism. The call for clear-cut policies, based on stands of principle, has never been met. The government's response has been to avoid broad commitments, to shape its policies according to changing circumstances and changing perceptions, and to limit its vision while picking its way gingerly through the South African minefield. This not only reflects the British style of decision-making but is seen in the government as a means of retaining both the economic advantages of the relationship and a reasonable consensus at home. To the committed it is at best a confused and incoherent response, and at worst hypocritical and against Britain's long-term interests. Yet major change is unlikely. There are too many differences of value and attitude, too many people with a stake in South Africa for that. If the government were to bow to its critics, it would have to give South Africa a much higher priority than it does at present, and to have the political will to stand against the tide of opposition that would come whatever its decisions. There is a paradox in this, for while South Africa gains great political attention, it is not perceived by the British government as a 'core interest'.[33] This would come about only if South Africa were to burst into such international prominence that there was a perceived major threat to British interests or the international system as a whole. As things stand, the internal situation in South Africa seems most likely to remain in what has been described as a state of 'violent equilibrium', in which neither the government nor the black nationalists are able to force a decisive conclusion.

The most likely mix of the British government's policies will still be in the 'constructive engagement'/'pressure for reform' range of options. This does not mean that there will not also be examples of 'cooperation' and 'confrontation'. The government's continuing support for economic links is certainly a form of cooperation, while, at the other end of the scale, no British government can entirely dismiss the possibility of imposing some form of economic sanctions. This might come about for three reasons: first, if the black states, aided by sympathetic allies, were able to organize effective economic action against Britain because of its connection with South Africa; second, if instability in southern Africa involving South Africa reached such a pitch that it threatened general international order, in which case sanctions might be used to try to force South Africa to comply with steps that would help restore that order; and, third, if, for these or other reasons, Britain's main Western partners decided to impose sanctions, making it difficult for Britain not to follow suit.

This last point is critical to understanding future British policy. The British government now sees itself as part of a Western team, which, by working together in southern Africa, gives each member more influence and more protection. A major priority for Britain must be to work in harness with its Western allies, and although there are periods, like that of the Reagan administration, when the pull is towards greater cooperation with South Africa, the general trend is the other way – to move Britain into a more critical stance than it might adopt if it were working alone.

Appendix: French and West German Relations with South Africa

by Christopher R. Hill

French and West German relations with South Africa have been chosen as the subject of this appendix because France and West Germany are Britain's major partners in the European Community (EC) and it has become an objective of British policy to 'spread the load' of relations with South Africa by acting as much as possible in concert with fellow members of the Community. France and Germany's relationships are still largely bilateral, but there are already two contexts within which they operate on a multilateral basis. First, both are members of the so-called Contact Group of five Western nations, which, since 1977, has negotiated with the Republic over Namibia; second, both, as members of the EC, take part in the developing process of European Political Cooperation (EPC). I shall begin with a brief discussion of the latter.

European Political Cooperation

The recent history of the EC's joint foreign policy towards southern Africa, developed within the framework of Political Cooperation, can be traced to the meeting of the nine foreign ministers at Luxembourg on 23 February 1976. Under the presidency of M. Gaston Thorn, then Luxembourg's foreign minister, they adopted a declaration which called for the cessation of all external military intervention in Angola, congratulated the OAU on its efforts to find an African solution there, asserted the Nine's readiness to develop cooperative relations to the extent desired by the African states, supported the right to self-determination of the Rhodesian and Namibian peoples, and condemned South Africa's policy of apartheid. The statement went on to say that although each state would recognize Angola individually, this would be done in a concerted manner, in order to demonstrate that it proceeded from a genuinely common will.

On 2 April 1976, there followed a further declaration on Rhodesia, and on 28 September 1976 the Dutch foreign minister, speaking as president of the Council of Ministers and of Political Cooperation, made a major speech at the United Nations on behalf of the Nine, which stated joint positions on Rhodesia, South Africa (including the 'purported independence' of the Transkei) and Namibia. A further statement on Rhodesia, in the fourth committee, was made by the Dutch on 8

December 1976, and on 31 December the nine foreign ministers issued a further statement, condemning the Smith regime in stronger terms than they had adopted before. Much more recently, the EC reacted to the South African attack on African National Congress (ANC) bases in Maputo.

The Commission of the European Communities (the EC's supranational civil service) also takes foreign policy initiatives, both on its own and in the form of proposals to the Council of Ministers, and it is clear, as Reinhardt Rummel has said, that with the growth of EPC there are evolving two sets of machinery within which European foreign policy is made, Political Cooperation and the Commission itself. He points to a 'marked decrease in the relative importance of treaty-based Community activity'. Political Cooperation, with its 'inclusion of considerable segments of the foreign offices and diplomatic service in other countries has resulted in relatively extensive coordination of national foreign policy to yield a European product'. The goal of the 'big three' and Italy is 'not so much to be subsumed by a new European identity, but rather better to defend their national interests through cooperation'.[1]

Rummel has thus put his finger on two sources of tension within the Community: first, between the Commission and Political Cooperation; second, between tendencies towards integration of foreign policy, as opposed to cooperation for the defence of separate national interests. A third area of tension becomes apparent when member states issue joint declarations, yet pursue a discernibly individual national interest. All three sources of disunity may be observed in the Community's dealings with South Africa, where the position is complicated further by the membership of the 'big three' in the Contact Group (originally the five Western states which were at that time members of the Security Council – Britain, France, Germany, the USA and Canada) which have been negotiating with South Africa over Namibia, and by the Community's need to demonstrate an acceptable South African policy in order to smooth its relations with its Third World partners in the renegotiated Lomé Convention, which runs from 1980 to 1985.[2]

Political Cooperation is conducted primarily in the capital of the country holding the presidency and, on occasions, in Brussels. In addition, there are frequent consultations among the Ten in other EC capitals. EPC also takes place in capitals of non-EC states, where ambassadors of the Ten, and other embassy staff, compare notes, exchange information and occasionally write joint reports. Such meetings occur in Pretoria (or Cape Town during the South African parliamentary session), but there EPC is somewhat overshadowed by the consultations within the Contact Group, though it retains a valuable function by providing a forum in which non-members of the five may be briefed on the Namibian negotiations. The 'front-line' position of the five in the Namibian question means that the involvement of other members of the EC is necessarily secondary and, since the question is seen as primarily political (whereas in the early days of the dispute it was approached by the United Nations as first and foremost a legal matter), the EC has not reached a group conclusion on certain aspects, of which perhaps the legal is the most important.

Germany and the Namibian question

In the past few years the West German government has developed a considerable interest in southern Africa and the Third World generally. This may be traced partly to the personal interest of Herr Hans-Dietrich Genscher, who has been foreign minister since 1974, but partly (so far as southern Africa is concerned) to the strong historical link between Germany and Namibia, and the continuing presence there of a sizeable German community.

When Herr Genscher moved to the Foreign Office in 1974, it seemed clear that if Germany was to play a distinctive part in world affairs it must do so in the Third World, for it did not seem that any great new initiatives would be possible in Ostpolitik or in the European and Atlantic partnerships, and Germany has not felt it could do much, beyond making supportive declarations, to assist a settlement in the Middle East. Thus, without departing from his deep commitment to a European, rather than a purely national, foreign policy, Herr Genscher has devoted many of his major speeches to his hopes for the peaceful resolution of conflict in the Third World.[3] It is also possible that, in concentrating on the Third World, he saw a way of differentiating himself from the chancellor, Herr Schmidt, who at that time took little interest in it.

Like the whole of Western Europe, Germany was alarmed by the disorderly transfer of power in Angola, and this, combined with the geographical proximity of Angola and Namibia, stimulated intense thought about southern Africa, both in the German government and, largely at its behest, in research foundations and other non-governmental bodies. On Namibia, far more detailed thinking has been done than on the remainder of southern Africa. Ministers are particularly exercised over the presence there of some 18,000 ethnic Germans (at the end of 1977), of whom 6,400 were German citizens, 1,600 had dual nationality and 10,000 were South Africans. (Many of the last category had renounced German nationality during the war, or were the children of parents who had done so.)

There has been on the whole a feeling of pessimism and dismay at the loss of political involvement in Africa (both actual and potential) which Germany would suffer if the initiative of the five came to nothing, as seemed only too likely after the abortive Geneva conference of January 1981. Opinion has, at least since 1979, been unanimous in the government that SWAPO must at all costs be included in the political process, though there is disagreement on the right wing of the CDU/CSU (Christian Democrats), which has been bitterly opposed to the Ministry of Foreign Affairs (not, as might be expected, the Ministry of Development) giving humanitarian aid to the liberation movements. Such aid, in Herr Strauss's view, made Germany an accessory to murder.[4]

Nevertheless, the German government is firm in its intention to liaise with all political forces in southern Africa, including the liberation movements. In this intention the FDP (Free Democrats), of which Herr Genscher is leader, and its coalition partner, the SPD (Social Democrats), are as one. The FDP election manifesto, adopted at its conference in Freiburg on 7 June 1980, stated: 'We support the initiative for the exercise of the right of self-determination in Namibia which is the result of a joint effort by the Federal Government and its principal allies.'[5] On 23 October 1980, Herr Genscher welcomed Mr Sam Nujoma, president of SWAPO, to a working dinner during his first visit to Germany. In his toast (for which he was later much criticized) he referred with pleasure to SWAPO's commitment 'to participate in free and fair elections in Namibia, under United Nations control and on the basis of Security Council Resolution 435. The affirmative attitude to this course of action constitutes an important affinity between SWAPO and the Federal Republic of Germany.' A subsequent press statement by the Federal Ministry for Economic Cooperation announced the offer, welcomed by Nujoma, to absorb into the existing southern African scholarship programme refugees hitherto in the care of SWAPO. However, perhaps the most important aspect of this visit, in view of the German sensitivity about the ethnic Germans in Namibia, was Nujoma's explicit reference to them as 'Namibian citizens of German origin'.[6]

Government policy was well summed up by Dr Uwe Holtz, an SPD member of the Bundestag and chairman of its Committee for Economic Cooperation, in a debate on 26 November 1980: 'The Federal Government seeks dialogue with all political forces in the south of the African continent, including the liberation movements, and it intends to continue energetically its endeavours to lead Namibia into internationally endorsed independence ... We recognize the liberation movements in southern Africa – such as ANC and SWAPO in Namibia – as important spokesmen of their peoples.'[7]

The West German commitment to Namibia was yet further indicated by Dr Hildegard Hamm-Brücher, Minister of State at the Ministry of Foreign Affairs, at a reception for African ambassadors in Bonn on 2 February 1981, when he referred to the 'important first meeting' which the government had arranged at the Geneva conference between SWAPO and 'Namibians of German descent which had resulted in a constructive exchange of ideas' and went on to refer to the Lomé Convention, to which, he emphasized, the door remained open for such African nations as had not yet decided to accede.[8]

No discussion of German views on Namibia can ignore the question of sanctions. These have been energetically discusssed, both in Bonn and in the Contact Group (indeed, at one point the South Africans believed their application to be imminent), and, although France, Britain and the USA jointly vetoed them at the UN Security Council in April 1981, it cannot be assumed that this weapon will remain indefinitely unused. Indeed, Germany has already introduced sanctions on a very limited scale, by making it known that when the South African military attaché in Bonn was replaced, his successor would not be given *agrément*.[9] One of the other sanctions discussed was the reduction of diplomatic representation to chargé d'affaires level, which could have been done without stirring up pro-South-African public opinion in Germany, whilst conveying an unmistakable signal of displeasure to the South African government. More serious measures could have included the abrogation of cultural and double taxation agreements and the temporary interruption of air traffic. Herr Genscher is reputed to have been in favour of the last, but to have failed to gain the support of other foreign ministers.

The problem, it is recognized, is to separate the question of Namibia from that of human rights in South Africa and to devise measures which will be specific, effective in a limited time, and reversible when the desired objective has been achieved. There is, of course, no unanimity on sanctions. On the one hand, it is thought that, when applied to South Africa itself, they might drive the Republic further into isolation, and that the Republic would be fortified in two ways: first, by its own conviction of moral virtue and, second, by the sympathy of many Germans, who accept the South African view that Germany is the only remaining considerable power to have a responsible public opinion which wishes to treat South Africa 'fairly'. On the other hand, a credible demonstration might encourage the *verligtes* (the 'enlightened' nationalists), though it has to be borne in mind that Hanf, in a study which is constantly quoted, has shown that by no means all the power establishment are *verlig*.[10]

The chancellor himself has spoken out in no uncertain terms against sanctions, apparently without any diminution of his influence or popularity in Africa. In Nigeria, in the autumn of 1978, he showed himself fully aware of the importance of Nigerian oil, but said unequivocally that there would be no sanctions against South Africa, and in Zambia he made a similar statement. Herr Loderer, president of the Metalworkers Union (and in 1979 of the International Metal Workers), also came out against sanctions after a visit to South Africa in 1978, having in the past been the only notable German trade unionist critic of South

Africa. Herr Genscher, it is thought, has favoured a forceful policy towards South Africa, but, except in the limited case of short-term measures relating to Namibia, would not go as far as sanctions; the economics minister is naturally cautious; the chancellor is thought, though against sanctions, to lean more towards the Genscher line. These nuances of difference are, in a sense, rendered irrelevant by the Western veto at the United Nations in April 1981, but they could acquire renewed importance when talk of sanctions becomes alive again, whether in the limited context of Namibia or as part of a campaign to secure changes in the Republic itself.

French views of Namibia

France lacks the Federal Republic's historical links with Namibia and has therefore played a less committed role in the Contact Group's negotiations. It has not diverged from the group's agreed policies, but it has, on the whole, left it to other members to make the running, which, so far as Europe is concerned, has left the leadership in British hands, though working in close collaboration with Germany.

Within the five there is, of course, some French jealousy of British influence in English-speaking Africa and a corresponding determination to deepen French contacts outside the Francophone region. The French also suspect (no doubt in part correctly) that the German involvement in the Namibian negotiations has been intended to secure minerals for the future and to regain influence in Africa.[11]

As far as sanctions are concerned, in view of the Western veto they are not an issue at present, but at an earlier stage they may well have been considered seriously in Paris (though with distaste) in the specific context of the Namibian initiative. There was, however, considerable scepticism about even Britain, with its special need to take initiatives, applying sanctions to persuade South Africa to alter its policies in the Republic itself. Since the French were determined that the lead must come from Britain or the USA, this scepticism reinforced the French policy of intelligent inactivity and, even if a lead had been given, France would by no means certainly have followed it, though it was recognized that ultimately sanctions might not be avoidable. The French would, however, have strenuously resisted any suggestion that the first sanctions should be nuclear, for if, as they believe is possible, South Africa has 'gone nuclear' (i.e. developed a bomb of its own), it has been with German and American help and the French see no reason why their sales of peacefully intended nuclear technology should be impeded. It appears that this attitude has been modified little, if at all, by the change of government in France.

Furthermore, the French find it difficult to take talk of sanctions seriously (except in the context of UN debates) in view of the trade which they are sure is carried on with South Africa by all black states which are able to pay for their purchases. Finally, if sanctions were efficiently applied, the first victim, in the French view, would be Mozambique. Thus, France had no difficulty in joining the USA and Britain in vetoing sanctions, and no doubt had fewer qualms than had its two partners over the Third World odium inevitably to be incurred by that action.

The accession to power of President Mitterrand has naturally raised questions in the minds of France's European partners and in South Africa. In South Africa there has been some alarm at the transition to a socialist government, with a minority of communist ministers. However, alarm was tempered by a number of realizations: South African coal heated French homes; South Africa had lived with left-wing governments in Europe before; France must beware of worsening its unemployment problem; the Koeberg nuclear power station contract (valued at 9 billion francs) was unlikely to be affected;[12] Mitterrand's campaign promise of sanctions against South Africa could be taken with a pinch of salt.[13]

There have, it is true, been hard-line statements by M. Lionel Jospin, secretary-general of the French Socialist Party (PS). The PS's policy, he said, at a conference on South Africa in Paris in April 1981, was to introduce sanctions, end all trade with Namibia, especially in uranium, run down imports from South Africa, introduce a total arms embargo, and end guarantees by COFACE (Compagnie Française d'Assurance pour le Commerce Extérieur – the French export guarantee agency) for exports to South Africa.[14] But M. Claude Cheysson, the new minister of external affairs (and lately Commissioner for Development in the European Commission), has been notably less specific. He refused to send an official delegation to the sanctions conference, on the ground that France was bound by the previous government's policies, and subsequently Minister Jean-Pierre Cot reiterated, at a press conference in Lagos, his government's scepticism about the efficacy of sanctions.[15] France would honour all existing arms contracts, but would seek to reduce South African imports, for example coal.

Further examination of M. Cheysson's remarks shows little difference in tone from those of his predecessor, M. Jean François-Poncet. The latter energetically defended, in parliament and the press, his government's decision to reintroduce visas for South Africans with effect from 1 September 1979, and then to refuse visas to the Springbok rugby team, giving as reasons the disgust caused by apartheid in Africa and the world at large and France's traditional abhorrence of racial discrimination. Under M. Giscard d'Estaing, COFACE did not guarantee commerce with Namibia; in July 1980 France unreservedly supported Security Council Resolution 435 on Namibia and M. François-Poncet received Sam Nujoma for 'very friendly talks' on 10 September, when he referred to the satisfactory relations between France and SWAPO and to the scholarships granted to young Namibians to study in France; he 'condemned the odious racial system that makes a mockery of human rights [and called on] the South African government to open a dialogue with those who are demanding recognition of their inalienable dignity'.[16] Like his successor, M. François-Poncet was cautious about sanctions, though he did not rule them out: 'I think we must be careful and see that sanctions do not bring about a result that could be the reverse of what we try to achieve.'[17]

Subsequently, M. Cheysson has confirmed that France's interests in Africa are not confined to those countries with which France has special relations. 'Africa has special relations, globally, with the Community of which we are members. Consequently, we shall have relations with the various African countries.'[18] He has said (no doubt in deference to the USA) that in Namibia 'there must, of course, be an evolution which respects the white minority', and he has echoed M. François-Poncet's doubts about sanctions (these remarks were made after the Security Council veto): 'When Rhodesia became independent, it had an industrial structure which would never have developed to that stage without the sanctions. So when, for South Africa, we go on to the next chapter, we must ask ourselves about the efficacy of economic sanctions. Of course there will be an arms boycott. France will not supply any arms, not one bolt, not one spare part to South Africa and she will not be alone in this.'[19] He somewhat modified this last commitment later, and made it clear that existing contracts, awkward though some might be, would be honoured on the ground that 'France does not have the right to go back on her signature'.[20]

Thus, French policy may well continue with little deflection from the previous government's line. If the Namibian negotiations are to succeed, the five need to hold together, and the French, who are as anxious as their colleagues that they should succeed, decided, after some hesitation, to continue to work within the Contact Group. Furthermore, the French are fully aware of Soviet interest in Francophone Africa and are unlikely to welcome an extension of their involvement in the southern region, particularly as President Mitterrand has no cause to love the Soviet Union, at whose hands he has suffered snubs never extended to his predecessor.

German relations with South Africa

As we have seen, German interest in southern Africa, with the exception of Namibia, is relatively new, and expertise, though growing, is not yet widespread. Germany's overall interests are to encourage change in the Republic, provided always that it be peaceful, to protect German citizens, investment, trade and mineral supplies, to maintain influence in the Third World by being seen to have an acceptable policy towards the Republic, and so far as possible to act in concert with other powers, rather than alone.

Whereas it has been accepted that Germany has a responsibility for Namibia, it has been felt, as in other countries, that officials should not think out possible future social and constitutional arrangements for South Africa, but should actively encourage others to undertake research. (In this connection one must note the far closer relationships which exist between research institutes and government in Germany than is usually the case in, for example, Britain.) Germany has, therefore, never tried to tell South Africa exactly what reforms it should introduce (though there are voices, of course, which urge that the Federal Republic and the West generally should do precisely that), but has limited itself to identifying goals. In this connection there have been long discussions with British and American colleagues as to whether those goals should include 'one man one vote in a unitary state'.

Some years ago Germany did present, though only orally, a list of goals to the South African government, and on subsequent occasions Herr Genscher has urged on his South African opposite number the need for progress in the Republic, if only in general terms. These goals included: the gradual abolition of apartheid; the gradual equal participation of the whole population in the social, economic and political fields (importance is attached to the order); the sharing of political responsibility and the acceptance of the principle of democratic majority rule. It seems likely that, although the general direction of desired change remains the same, Germany would now attach rather less emphasis to the achievement of particular targets.

Public opinion

In general, it may be said that 'orthodox' establishment opinion on South Africa in Germany is somewhat to the right of that obtaining in Britain, particularly in the business community, whose acceptance of its social responsibilities is less noticeable than in Britain. There is, too, far greater acceptance of the proposition that it is not for government to interfere more than is absolutely essential in business matters, and very strong resistance is made by business to any measures which extend the role of government or tend to politicize economic affairs.

All in all, particularly in view of Germany's position as a front-line state in Europe, it is hardly surprising that liberal thinking should be rather less widespread than in Britain, and policy less ostentatiously pro-African than was the case under the British Labour government. Certainly, there is no lack of pro-South-African feeling in Bonn; the South African Embassy propagandizes energetically and successfully, and sometimes advertisements appear over the South African government's name which use quite undiplomatic language and would in Britain be left to some such body as the Club of Ten. There is as well a strong lobby, mostly in the parliamentary opposition, with some links to the business world, which opposes the government's 'appeasement' policies in Africa and berates it for its friendly relations with oppressive and dictatorial regimes throughout Africa and, in Namibia, for preparing to give away to the communist-backed SWAPO everything that Germans have built up, endangering thousands of German lives in the process. On the left, in addition to those specifically involved in anti-apartheid work, there are groups of students and Third World specialists who regularly write to ministers complaining that policy is not liberal enough, and these enjoy the sympathy of left-wing SPD members of parliament, who, however, play little, if any, part in the process of foreign-policy-making.

Though the ANC is not yet represented in Germany (it has considered opening an office in Frankfurt), there is an effective Anti-Apartheid Movement which shares a building with ISSA (Informationstelle Südliches Afrika), a serious body producing a number of 'committed' and well-researched publications. (ISSA is accepted by government as a suitable alternative employment for young people who object on conscientious grounds to national service.) In establishment circles the AAM is extremely suspect, because of its alleged communist connections, a natural enough reaction in a divided Germany. One must also not forget that, in attacking capitalism for its support of South African racism, the AAM strikes at the heart of West German identity, and in presenting capitalists as racists it touches a nerve which is still raw, thirty-eight years after the war.

Cultural relations and development aid

There is a long tradition of German-language education in South Africa, because of the long-established German-speaking community there. There are six German private schools (two-thirds of whose income comes in the form of subsidy by the German government), of which the four most important are at Johannesburg (1,600 pupils), Cape Town (500), Pretoria (500) and Hammelsburg (300). These four take pupils as far as matriculation; the others stop at standards V and VI. There are also a number of smaller schools which receive no subsidy, but which may send their better pupils on to one of the 'big four'.

The German government is now opening these schools to 'non-whites' despite some white parental opposition. A start has been made at Cape Town, with concentrated instruction in German language in standards IV–VI. The lead was given by the Roman Catholic church, which expected legislation to be passed in 1977 to permit private schools to integrate. When this failed to materialize, they went ahead nevertheless, with the agreement of the Administrator of the Cape, and under the blind eye of the *verkrampte* (hard-line) Administrator of the Transvaal. At the beginning of 1979 there had been a total of about 1,000 non-white children in all white private schools: roughly 400 each in the Cape and Natal, 200–300 in the Transvaal, and none in the Orange Free State. By October 1981 there were 566 non-white pupils taking German-language courses preparatory to entering the German schools alone. In 1981 expenditure envisaged under the Federal government's special cultural programme for southern Arica was DM1.5m, which, it was hoped, would increase to approximately DM3m in 1982. The bulk of the expenditure was to go on providing further education for black secondary school teachers of science subjects in Soweto, and scholarships for talented non-white secondary pupils. The practical implementation of the programmes had been handed over to independent non-governmental organizations.

There is a small programme of visits by South Africans to West Germany arranged through the Federal Press and Information Office: originally intended for journalists, the programme has now been extended to a few trade unionists, partly, at least, because journalists are scarce. Germany already offers scholarships through the Deutsche Akademische Austausch Dienst and the Hilbrandt Foundation. In the early 1970s there was a great shortage of blacks of the required academic standard, since to be granted a scholarship they had first to have been accepted for an MA. In 1971 three scholarships were given to blacks and eight to whites; in 1979, thanks partly to faithful advisers in the universities, it became possible for the German Embassy in Pretoria to allow for a maximum of twelve blacks and six whites, the latter with extremely high qualifications.

One important avenue for German cultural, and hence political, influence in South Africa, is through the churches. These have great wealth, since a proportion of the individual's income tax is earmarked for his church (if he has no church he pays correspondingly less tax), and private gifts to religious causes are tax-deductible. Consequently, both black and white churches receive considerable financial support from Germany, and the funds of the South African Council of Churches (SACC) come largely from there. The SACC is a lively and influential body. One cannot evaluate how much its predominantly German funding promotes specifically German influence in the religious, cultural and political fields, but the influence is not all one way. The SACC firmly believes that it must not merely seek to alleviate conditions in South Africa, but must educate Germans about their own involvement in the oppression of non-whites. It is not enough for the SACC simply to take German money: there must also be informed discussion of, for example, the churches' investment in companies with South African connections.[21] The SACC believes that if the churches fail in their search for justice, they will simply drive committed Christians into opposition to the established churches or into Marxism. The latter, with its holistic explanation of all human phenomena, is seen as a real danger, particularly to the young. And it is the young who are not represented in church governing bodies, but are often spoken for by the middle-aged and middle-class.

Although there is considerable church aid, there is no German official aid to South Africa, since it is not classed as a developing country, and the German government is determined that this policy will not change, however worthy the black organizations which might receive it. Formerly the Bundesministerium für Zusammenarbeit (BMZ – the equivalent of the British Overseas Development Administration) sent about DM7m a year to such bodies as the Christian Institute, but since these bodies have been rendered ineffective by the South African government, the subventions ended at the end of 1977. There is here some difference of emphasis between the British and German governments, since the last British government decided to establish a small aid scheme, and its Conservative successor confirmed the decision shortly after the election of 1979.[22]

Germany is well aware that any development policy in black Africa requires OAU cooperation, which must be safeguarded by an acceptable policy in South Africa. It is thought that Germany's present relations with South Africa do not impede good relations with black Africa, though any military or nuclear cooperation would. (This may explain the German government's publication in October 1978 of a detailed rebuttal of accusations of such cooperation, made by the ANC, the Anti-Apartheid Movement and others.[23]) It was acknowledged that the passage to Rhodesia of vehicles exported to South Africa did harm Germany's standing in black Africa, but there was no action the German government could take, since the vehicles were not of a specifically military kind.

No official aid goes to Namibia (though the CSU's Foundation in Munich is said to have supported the Democratic Turnhalle Alliance), nor will any, unless Namibia receives international recognition. However, there are considerable quantities of 'unofficial' aid through charitable and religious organizations. For example, it is widely believed that the Konrad Adenauer Stiftung, the Deutsche Afrika Stiftung (which is run from the opposition's secretariat) and the Heinrich Seidel Stiftung were all involved in support for the DTA. Meanwhile, as we have seen, the German government has extended its scholarship programme to Namibian refugees.

Although Germany has an active overseas aid programme (both officially and through foundations, whose role in this and other fields is of the greatest importance), officials are very exercised about how much of the aid budget should be spent in educating the German public. A BMZ survey showed that 37 per cent of the public believed development aid to be necessary (though many of these were uninformed and it is not clear how many thought aid good, as well as necessary), 25 per cent were against aid, and 38 per cent were indifferent or knew nothing about it.

Minerals

Like all industrial states, Germany is a great consumer of mineral resources. A committee of State Secretaries (equivalent of British Permanent Under-Secretaries) started work in July 1978, and reported in November, on an evaluation of Germany's need for South African minerals and, not surprisingly, came to the conclusion that they were absolutely essential in the short term, though in the long term dependence could be reduced by recycling, substitution and diversification of sources of supply.[24]

The main conclusion was that certain minerals (chrome, vanadium, manganese, blue asbestos and cobalt from Zaire) must be stockpiled as the only short-term defence against interruptions in supply. It was emphasized, however, that this decision should not be seen as the prelude to sanctions, but as an indication that in the longer term South Africa represented a political risk. No attempt was made to involve EC partners in the full investigation (though there were limited discussions) because it was felt that national supply systems differed too much to make detailed cooperation useful, and in general that other member states were not yet ready to carry out such an investigation. Industry and government both believed that a one year stockpile should be accumulated, and the committee inclined to the view that the scheme should be run by government and industry in cooperation, though there was some doubt about which industrial enterprises should be chosen, and how the interests of smaller enterprises should be safeguarded. The decision to stockpile was taken in principle in June 1979: however, it appears that the difficulties of funding (the sum of one billion DM was envisaged) have led to the plans being shelved, despite regret in military quarters.

The available figures are rather meagre; a report published in 1979 by the Federal Minister of Economics (Bundesminister für Wirtschaft – BMWI), the minister responsible for the encouragement of exploration for minerals, gives few details of German consumption, but states that Germany depends 100 per cent on imports of tin, aluminium, nickel, tungsten and phosphate, 98 per cent for iron ore, 99–100 per cent for copper, 87 per cent for lead and 65 per cent for zinc. Germany accounts for roughly 7 per cent of world consumption of aluminium, lead, copper, zinc, tin and nickel (unfortunately no breakdown between the metals is given), and in 1976 it depended directly upon South Africa for 13 per cent of its copper imports, and 11 per cent of its zinc.[25] In 1979 Germany was the second most important market, by value, for South African minerals (excluding gold), taking 18 per cent of exports, behind only Japan, which took 20 per cent.[26]

As the BMWI report says, 'owing to political developments in South Africa', Germany has for some years been making considerable efforts to diversify its supply of chrome, and several projects have been started in Brazil and the Philippines. German consortia are participating in large projects in Papua New Guinea and Fiji. But exploration (aided by the government's exploration subsidy programme) continues in South Africa, where deposits of fluorspar and titanium magnetite have been found, but are not being developed because shipment is possible only through Mozambique. During 1973–7 one credit guarantee was given for a mineral project in South Africa. It appears that in 1979 Germany succeeded in significantly reducing its dependence on South African chrome, with 48 per cent of its requirements (66 per cent in 1978), manganese 52 per cent (73 per cent) and blue asbestos 66 per cent (88 per cent) coming from the Republic.[27]

The study prepared for the BMWI on the risk of interruption of supplies for political reasons (of whatever kind) made it possible to work out a classification (it is not clear whether this was done in the ministry itself) ranking minerals according to risk factor in scale 500–100. Chrome was easily the most at risk, with 365, followed by: manganese 300, asbestos 298, niobium 295, tungsten 288, cobalt 283, vanadium 281, titanium 278, platinum 270, and boron 256. The lowest of the 28 ranked was barite, which scored 107: that is, virtually nil risk.

A further study asked the likely effect on production overall in Germany if mineral imports were cut by 30 per cent. In answering the question, it became clear that some materials, like manganese, imported in small quantity, were as important for the economy as, for example, copper, whether the effect on production or on jobs was being considered. The State Secretaries' committee accepted that a 30 per cent reduction in chrome imports could reduce overall German production by 25 per cent and endanger several million jobs, to greater or lesser degree. Above all, the committee concluded, the raw materials policy must seek to protect the stainless steel sector.[28]

The Code of Conduct

The robust individuality of German business is well illustrated by the difficulty the government has experienced over the EC's Code of Conduct for firms with interests in South Africa. The current position is that all companies which receive Hermes financing (equivalent of British Export

Credit Guarantees) for exports to South Africa must, whether or not they have subsidiaries there, sign a declaration that they know and approve of the statement issued jointly by the Bund der Deutschen Industrie (BDI, the equivalent of the Confederation of British Industry), the Deutsche Industrie und Handelstag (the German Chamber of Trade and Industry – DIHT), and the Afrika Verein (an association of firms with interests in Africa) after a meeting on 27 September 1977 with the State Secretary of the Ministry of Foreign Affairs, who, confusingly, was Herr Hermes (he subsequently became ambassador in Washington). The statement says that the parties approve the political aims of the code and are willing to see that its general principles are translated into practice.

The agreement was reached after a long tussle over article 7 of the code, which concerns reporting. The initial proposal made by the business organizations was that companies would each write a report for the Association of Commerce and Industry, which in turn would write a general report for submission to the government. This was not acceptable to the government, which feared the possible adverse effect on public opinion – and long negotiations ensued, lasting from August 1978 until February 1979. It was finally agreed that individual companies would report directly to the Ministry of Economics, which would then produce a general report. Business has consistently opposed following the British practice whereby individual companies' reports are published, although some companies, like Siemens, do, in fact, publish individual 'social reports'; but among the smaller ones, some of which have so far managed to keep off the lists compiled at the United Nations, there are fears of undesirable publicity and of retaliation by anti-apartheid groups. The government's first report under the code was eventually published on 16 January 1980, and drew on material from 46 companies, employing 30,488 people – about 90 per cent of all employees of German firms in South Africa.[29]

For a number of reasons the government feels in a weak position and, since the code is voluntary, can, like other governments, only persuade, rather than require, companies to comply.[30] (However, the British government's powers of persuasion appear greater, or its political will stronger.) Above all, there is a lack of information. There exists no law whereby companies must register their activities abroad, and the introduction of such a law would be anathema to them, so that the question has never been raised. Transfer of capital abroad is registered only for the compilation of statistics of capital flows; the transferor need not even state the name of the transferee, and any attempt to extract information about individual companies would transgress the law relating to statistics. There is thus no easy means available in Bonn of compiling a list of companies with subsidiaries in South Africa, though, of course, the German Embassy in

Pretoria will be expected to obtain such relevant information as it can, and membership of the South African–German Chamber of Trade and Industry may readily be gleaned in Johannesburg from perusal of the Chamber's publications.

It might be thought that names of companies with interests in South Africa could be gathered from the list of those receiving Hermes guarantees. This has, however, not been tried, and in any case would not yield information as to the recipients' interests there, since the guarantees are for payment for exports. To make such inquiries might also undermine confidence in the Hermes system as a whole, whose purposes are economic rather than political.

The Hermes conditions vary from country to country. Exporters to South Africa may receive guarantees of up to DM50m per contract, provided that each contract is with a different firm in South Africa. Hermes financing has never been given or withheld on political grounds, and it is clear that the strength of German business is such that the government would hesitate to use this weapon to obtain compliance with the code. Any such decision would very definitely be taken at political, rather than official, level.

The BDI's attitude to the Code of Conduct and to the negotiations which preceded its adoption in Germany is naturally different from that of the government. For example, exception is taken to the fact that it was announced without previous consultation with industry and, in explaining the long period occupied by the negotiations, emphasis is placed upon the differences between federal ministries, the Ministry of Economics having been, as one would expect, rather more cautious in its approach than was the Foreign Office. It is also pointed out that the code itself is more suitable to British than to German conditions and that part of the delay may be accounted for by the government's wish to find out, before concluding the negotiations, how successfully the code was being implemented in other countries, notably Britain. A further cause for concern is that American and Japanese firms are not bound by the code – and it may well be that some firms would lose their competitive position, or even collapse, if they were obliged to raise wages by, say, 20 per cent. (It is worth noting that even firms which have an above average record may have surprising blind spots. For example, Siemens, which pays subsistence level + 50 per cent, uses as its yardstick the minimum subsistence level for a family of only three persons, on the curious ground that that is in fact the average size of a black family in Siemens, because so many bachelors are employed.) There is also fairly widespread reluctance to report under the various headings used in the code and in the British scheme, since it is thought that a simple assurance that the principles of the code are being followed should be enough. Some businessmen think

British business was foolishly weak in agreeing to report in detail, but what form the German companies' reports actually take is not publicly known.

The 'politicization' of the Hermes system of guarantees is deplored in business circles, though it is recognized that in the current climate of disapproval of South Africa it cannot be reversed. This disapproval is itself deplored: it is believed both that the gradual liberalization of Eastern Europe owes much to the pioneering achievement of businessmen in the establishment of good working relationships, and that much of the odium reserved for South Africa should be directed against the Soviet bloc. Again, given the recent history of Germany, such a feeling is not surprising.

Some German firms are loath to reveal the extent of their holdings in South African subsidiaries, and the German government cannot oblige them to do so. Others regard the code as unnecessary, since they have always done their best for their black employees. Nor is the code widely seen as a device which will buy time for South Africa, and therefore (one would have thought) as a desirable measure. One influential view is that, in any case, South Africa has plenty of time, provided that Western governments and companies recognize that it lies in their own hands to maintain South Africa as a country where investments are safe. This must be done by, on the one hand, bringing black African states to accept (because they are powerless to change it) the state of affairs in South Africa and to retain their good relationships with the West, whilst at the same time persuading South Africa, by example rather than precept, that 'progressive' measures may safely be introduced. The extent to which business fears Soviet intervention in southern Africa, and eventually in the Republic itself, should also be noted.

The BDI has not held discussions with trade unions on South Africa, though the evolution of Herr Loderer's opinions has been noted with interest. In the report in which Herr Loderer came out against sanctions, his union urged the government to put strong pressure on firms to comply with the code.[31] Within the organization, however, it is feared that the EC code might become a precedent, and that other codes might be devised for other countries, endangering the export trade on which Germany is so dependent. Indeed, BDI representatives have made it clear to South African members of parliament and to homeland leaders that, in the BDI's view, it is the South African politicians' responsibility to ensure good business practices and so to release the German firms from the obligation to report.

The independent attitude of the business community extends even to the arms embargo, the administration of which is not altogether easy for the German government. The original list of goods for which an export licence must be sought was drawn up as long ago as 1963, with exports to the Soviet bloc in mind. (The latest version of this list is in an annexure to Bundesanzeiger 246 of 30 December 1976.) Thereafter, a few items (the list is not available) were added specifically in connection with South Africa, to comply with UN Resolution 418. Exporters who wish to export anything on the list will simply not seek to do so if Eastern Europe is the destination, since they know that permission will not be forthcoming. But for South Africa there are borderline cases, since items which *can* be used for military purposes (like Mercedes vehicles) are not solely and specifically made for military use, and so are not embargoed. Furthermore, certain items (like certain kinds of bearings) may not be exported to Eastern Europe, but, since that prohibition was not imposed for military reasons, it is not extended to South Africa.

The inability to control the purposes to which items not on the embargo list are eventually put in South Africa should be seen within the wider context of relations between business and government in Germany. There is strong opposition to any extension of regulation of exports, so that if government wishes to regulate foreign trade it must prove its case. In the United States, on the other hand (or at least in German perceptions of the USA), there is the opposite assumption that government has a right to regulate all foreign trade, unless it specifies areas in which it does not wish to intervene.

Investment

Great difficulties attend the compilation of statistics of investment in South Africa. Statistics have been kept since 1952 of the outflow of capital, but none of reinvestment of retained profit, nor, of course, of capital raised in third countries by South African subsidiaries of German companies, especially Eurocurrency loans or those obtained in the 'grey' market. Bearing all this in mind, German officials guessed direct investment at the end of 1978 at ±DM650m, which, according to the Federal Ministry of Economics, rose to DM678m in 1980.[32]

According to the Chamber of Trade and Industry, there was more direct than indirect new investment in 1976 and 1977 – otherwise they have been about even. Soweto (1976) had virtually no effect on direct investment, but it had some on portfolio investment. No firms moved out in 1978, and only two or three new ones came in, but great interest was shown at the investment seminars which the Chamber held in Germany in October 1978, mostly by medium-sized firms with DM5–10m to spend. They were impressed by the high profits obtainable, which made it possible to recover initial outlay in two or three years, and, perhaps for this reason, asked no questions about the political situation. They did, however, show interest in exchange control, which has, of course, been greatly liberalized as a result of the publication – also in 1978 – of the De Kock Commission's Report.

In 1979 a new statistical procedure was introduced which did not merely, as hitherto, measure capital transactions, but also included the book values of investments in subsidiaries abroad. The first results obtained under the new arrangements covered the year 1976 and were published by the Federal German Bank.[33] This publication defines direct investment as that part of the nominal capital and reserves of an undertaking abroad which belongs to a German parent company or individuals, as well as all credits and loans which the parent has made. To count as direct investment, at least 25 per cent of the subsidiary's nominal capital, or of the voting rights, must belong to the parent. Direct investment is divided into that made directly from parent to subsidiary and that made via a subsidiary holding company (that is, one in which the parent has at least a 50 per cent interest). The figures, it is pointed out, are produced in accordance with different accounting practices in many different countries, so that comparisons between countries may be inaccurate. The figures should also be regarded as, on the whole, representing the lowest value which could be attached to direct investments.

The new measure yields a figure of DM994m direct investment in South Africa, of which only DM114m went through intervening subsidiaries. It is based on returns by 187 companies (excluding subsidiary holding companies) employing 33,000 people. Companies with balance sheets of under DM500,000 are excluded. The data are given to the Bundesbank under conditions of complete secrecy and there is no way in which the German Foreign Office or any other Department of State could extract from the statistics any particulars of individual firms or individuals.

Clearly, no more accurate estimate of direct investment is likely to become available. Even greater difficulty comes when an attempt is made to compute total investment, including direct, indirect (including portfolio) and pre-1952 investment and reinvested profits. The Chamber records that guesses range between DM4,000 million and 12,000 million,[34] though by 1980 it had reduced the estimate to DM4,000–8,000 million.[35] (DM4,000 million would be about 8.4 per cent of total foreign investment in South Africa.)

With regard to bank loans, according to the Chamber's 1977–8 *Annual Report*,[36] South Africa's ability to raise money in the international money market was improving, though even in 1978 it had not been able to raise all the foreign capital it needed. In November 1978 it was possible, for the first time in over two years, to place a South African government loan, with some German participation, of $150m in the Eurodollar market, and several smaller ones to such bodies as Escom (Electricity Supply Commission), with maximum terms variously stated as six or six and a half years. A loan led by the Bayerische Vereinsbank at the end of 1978 had been for six years, whilst at the beginning of the year the term had been only three and a half: the extended term clearly indicates an important increase in foreign confidence. In October 1979 the South African Post Office raised DM50m for six years at $8\frac{1}{4}$ per cent, which appears to have been the best terms obtained in Germany since 1975.[37]

Early in 1980 Dr Alfred Herrhausen, a managing director of the Deutsche Bank, urged South Africa to borrow, even if it was not really necessary, in order to keep its name before world capital markets. He stated that the Deutsche Bank had directly lent R240m to South Africa and was involved to about the same amount in association with other banks. The bank was a big seller of kruggerrands, well over a million a year, which were sold through Luxembourg to avoid the German 13 per cent turnover tax.[38] In June 1980 the Deutsche Bank led a loan of DM120m for seven years at 9 per cent.[39]

The Chamber endorses figures originally produced by the United Nations Centre on Apartheid. According to the Centre's report, South Africa raised 158 foreign public sector loans to the value of US$5,500 million in the years 1972–8. Seventy-two of these loans, in which 59 banks were involved, originated in Germany.[40]

Trade
Germany's share of the South African market in the 1930s averaged about 8 per cent. After the war it was negligible, but it more than recovered by the mid-1950s, achieving rapid penetration until 1958. Thereafter it

Table 1   South African imports and exports in R million, 1979

		Imports	% change		Exports	% change
West Germany	(1)	1,308	+ 2.7	(5)	909	+ 33.4
Britain	(2)	1,253	+20.1	(3)	964	− 23.7
USA	(3)	1,240	+25.7	(2)	1,405	+ 4.1
Japan	(4)	800	− 2.8	(4)	949	+ 24.0
France	(5)	471	− 0.9	(7)	300	+ 18.8
Italy	(6)	250	+13.3	(6)	341	+ 70.9
Switzerland	(7)	181	+ 8.4	(1)	1,541	+331.6

Notes: (*a*) South Africa's total foreign trade was DM1,600m imports (excluding military goods and oil), and DM2,100m exports (including krugerrands, but excluding gold), of which the above seven countries accounted for 78.3 per cent and 68.3 per cent, respectively.

         (*b*) South Africa's favourable trade balance, its first in 25 years, is attributable largely to the greatly increased sales of krugerrands and, in the case of Switzerland particularly, to changes in the diamond trade.

Source: South African–German Chamber of Trade and Industry, *Annual Report 1980*, pp. 40–1.

remained static for ten years, and since then has climbed steadily to its present level. In the 1930s 10 per cent of South African exports went to Germany (though the figure rose to 19 per cent in 1938); after the war it was 6–7 per cent until the early 1970s, when it rose to about 10 per cent.[41] In 1979 West Germany became South Africa's most important source of imports and fifth export market.

In 1980 South African exports to Germany rose to DM3,262m, and imports to DM4,595m. (These compare with German imports from Nigeria of DM5,513m, and exports of DM3,320m.)[42] As one might expect, the exchange of goods is asymmetrical. Germany's imports include a high proportion of minerals and raw materials, whilst 96 per cent of its exports are finished goods.

Conclusion

We have seen that West Germany is heavily engaged with South Africa at both the political and the economic levels. German economic purposes are to maintain and extend trade, to safeguard investment and, above all, to ensure the continuing supply of essential minerals. The economic and political levels meet in the EC's Code of Conduct, which (despite protests by business at the politicization of economic relations) has enabled the governments of Western Europe, acting together, to make a significant gesture towards change in the Republic, without endangering any vital interest.

At the political level, West Germany has a special historical connection with Namibia, and the part played in the Federal Republic's policy by the need to compete world-wide with East Germany should never be forgotten.[43] However, though West Germany is determined to demonstrate that it has a morally based policy of its own in southern Africa, the bulk of its activity in relation to South Africa has been multilateral rather than bilateral: indeed, this emphasis on multilateralism is a feature of West German foreign policy world-wide.

French policy towards South Africa

In general, both France and Germany are content to let Britain make the running with South Africa, for a variety of reasons. Much depends on the level of expertise. In France, as is constantly emphasized by French officials, there is a very small pool of detailed knowledge of southern Africa and rather little research is being undertaken. Rhodesia was seen as a primarily British problem; Namibia, where, it is true, there are some French mining interests, has been handled largely in the Contact Group. Both these are regarded as problems of the end of the colonial era, whilst South Africa is a question of an entirely different type. It is not yet, however, a matter of urgency to think ahead to the means of dealing with it.

France, unlike Germany, though willing to set its hand to joint declarations, shows little interest in the formulation and carrying out of cooperative policies.[44] Disagreements between France and Germany were becoming apparent by 1979. The Germans saw continuing colonialism in the tight hold retained by France on Francophone Africa ('Francophoney' is a German joke), where the French protect mineral interests to the exclusion of those of their EC partners, while the French, as we have seen, in turn suspected that the German involvement in the Namibian negotiations had been intended to secure minerals for the future and to regain influence in Africa.

Between Britain and France the rivalry and distrust which are so noticeable in the EC institutions and activities can also be seen in relation to South Africa. Fortified by its relative independence of South African minerals,[45] France has made the political judgement that South Africa is not an immediate problem, so that policies designed to promote social change in South Africa need not be given any very high priority. Since Britain (and Germany) have made a very different political judgement and are both highly dependent on South African minerals, it is reasonable to expect British relations with France on the whole question of South Africa to continue in their present state of irritable frustration on the British side and comparative lack of interest on the French, and to deteriorate as competition for alternative sources of minerals intensifies.

Actions taken by France against South Africa include its refusal, operating within the framework of Political Cooperation, to recognize the 'independence' of the Transkei and Bophutatswana. Furthermore, France has subscribed to the EC Code of Conduct for firms operating in South Africa; on 4 November 1977 it voted for the Security Council resolution to impose a total embargo on sales of arms to South Africa (since a presidential decision of autumn 1976 a partial embargo had been in operation, which excluded naval contracts already in progress), and in 1979 the President himself decided against a tour of France which the Springboks were to have made in the autumn. Thus, under Giscard, France had to some extent, though very cautiously, shifted its South African policy. Its sensitivity, however, to Third World pressures on southern African issues is far less than is Britain's, partly because there is no tradition in France of involvement with the region, and partly because France is not particularly hard pressed in this regard by the Third World states with which it is most intimately linked, the Francophone states of West Africa. Though these would, all things being equal, like to see France distance itself from South Africa, they are not, as Lefort points out,[46] anxious to see it allied with liberation movements that are heavily influenced by the Soviet Union or China. But it appears that in the case of the Springbok tour (which caused real difficulties in Franco/South African relations), the Francophone states did feel obliged to exert pressure. Some more assertive policy may perhaps be expected under President Mitterrand, but, as has been argued in the section on Namibia, the extent of the change may well be limited.

Investment

Though France has no political interests in South Africa peculiar to itself, it does have investment and trade. Reliable investment figures are, however, even more difficult to come by than in other countries, not only because of the sensitivity of the whole South Africa question, but partly because French government and business circles are reluctant to publicize investment anywhere abroad in view of high unemployment in France and the difficulty of explaining to trade unions why foreign investment is necessary for the good of the economy as a whole.

Some estimates of investment have been made by the Centre Français du Commerce Extérieur (CFCE), which dwells on the difficulties in a briefing paper for businessmen interested in South Africa. Apart from the problem of definition, there is a statistical difficulty, which is encountered by anyone seeking figures relating to individual EC states' investment in South Africa,[47] because since 1973 the South African Reserve Bank no longer publishes the figures (though, of course, it possesses them) for individual member states of the EC. (Similarly, the USA is lost in a general 'America' category, but here the difficulty is smaller, since the USA is naturally the dominant component of that category.) There are the further difficulties, not peculiar to South Africa, that some capital transfers are made through third countries and that the statistics do not reveal how much self-financing is included.

Nevertheless, the CFCE does, by methods which it does not explain, come to the conclusion that total French investment in South Africa in 1975 was F736m (4.5 per cent of total foreign investment there), of which R139m was direct (R96m in 1966) and R597m (far more sharply up, from only R105m in 1966) indirect.[48] The French anti-apartheid movement (CRIAA) estimated French investment at 6 per cent of the total from abroad.[49]

Trade

Trade figures are much easier, since the Ministère du Budget publishes details of all French imports and exports, both by country and in an enormous number of categories and sub-categories. The trade figures are, however, not complete, since sales of military equipment, or of licences for local manufacture in South Africa of military hardware, are not included. Lefort puts them between F1.25bn and F2bn from 1970 to 1975, inclusive.[50]

As authorities as far apart as CFCE and the Anti-Apartheid Movement point out, France has unhesitatingly entered into contracts with South Africa at which its competitors jibbed. For example, Escom gave the French consortium of Framatone, Alsthom and Spiebatignolles the contract (said to be worth F9,000m[51]) for the Koeberg nuclear installation in May 1976, the Germans having withdrawn for political reasons, though they did share with the French the lion's share of the Koeberg extension, the total cost of which was estimated at F1,900m.[52] France has supplied four Airbuses, sold ships (one, for which the contract was cancelled, went to Argentina instead), built a railway, helped develop Richards Bay and greatly increased its imports of coal and uranium. Although, according to CRIIA,[53] M. de Guiringaud had said in Mozambique that he hoped his southern African journey would discourage French industrialists from investing in South Africa, a few months later they had the biggest stand at the Rand show, and were exchanging more trade missions than ever.

There are several reasons why investment in, and trade with, South Africa are barely a political problem in France. First, the French policy of diversification means that France would not be crippled if supplies in any one category were suddenly cut off (though in the short term the loss of, e.g., South Africa's coal or uranium would impose grave difficulties). Thus, France need not fear the effects of South African reprisals against possible UN sanctions in the future, but can continue its trade for the time being, whilst continuing prudently to diversify, but without devoting any great effort to long-term policy formulation. Compare this with the need imposed on Britain – by the combination of very great South African interests and sensitivity to Third World pressure – somehow to combine protection of those interests with a degree of responsiveness to pressure.

Secondly, because France has no traditional political links with South

Table 2 French trade with South Africa, 1973–80, in F million

	French exports	% change	French imports	% change
1973	1,071		980	
1974	1,678	+ 56.7	1,203	+31.1
1975	1,815	+ 8.2	1,234	+ 2.6
1976	2,320	+ 27.8	1,538	+24.6
1977	2,438	+ 5.1	2,470	+60.6
1978	2,723	+ 11.7	3,401	+37.7
1979	2,247	− 17.5	4,044	+18.9
1980	4,071	+ 81.2	4,071	+25.8
1981	5,435	+ 33.5	5,849	+15.0

Source: Conseil National du Patronat Français and *Statistiques du Commerce Extérieur de la France 1981*, produced by Ministère du Budget, Direction Générale des Douanes et Droits Indirects.

Africa and its vital interests are only peripherally involved, the pool of South African expertise in Paris is both small and relatively new. Even the pro-South-African lobby exists (it is said) as a by-product of anti-Soviet feeling or of the 'new right' in domestic politics. The former president himself never faced the problem of South Africa (though he was said to have a personal distaste for its policies), but he was heavily engaged with France's own intractable problems in West Africa, and it seems likely that the balance of President Mitterrand's attention will be similar. It is true that the French government is worried that the spread of the English language will eclipse French and therefore is seeking to diversify its contacts with Anglophone Africa, whilst at least claiming to welcome increased English penetration of the former French colonies. But this is a policy for black Africa: cultural links with South Africa are slight (fifteen scholarships, three lecturers in 'non-white' universities in 1979 with two more planned for 1980, the appointment of a cultural councillor in the Embassy in 1976, for the first time) and are likely so to remain.

Third, though French policy-makers and businessmen are as capable as anyone else of seeing that a period of chaos and war in southern Africa could be disastrous for the West, there seems to be no very widespread feeling that anything of the kind is at all likely in the near or medium-term future. As one senior official put it: 'The specificity of the South African question will take a long time to show itself, though it is specific, because it is not (unlike Rhodesia and Namibia) part of the colonial question. Meanwhile the problem of South Africa is one with which France can live.' It follows that, although the changed political climate, both in South Africa and internationally, must be taken into account by the intending investor, it should not necessarily dissuade him. The first essential, as CFCE points out, is to look carefully at a project's amortization period.[54]

Finally, trade with South Africa has in part been stimulated by a feeling in business circles that the continuing imbalance since 1977 is unhealthy.

Table 3   Major French imports from South Africa, 1980

Customs category	Shortened title	Value in F million
27	Combustibles	1,936.9
28	Inorganic chemical products	1,291.4
71	Pearls, precious stones and metals	386.3
26	Metal ores, slag and ash	417.4
53	Wool, animal hair and horsehair	227.1
08	Fruit	249.1
	TOTAL	4,508.2

Source: Statistiques du Commerce Extérieur de la France, 1980.

CFCE pointed out that the 1977 and earlier figures contained the benefit of major contracts, whose repetition could not be expected, so that a downward export trend must be foreseen, though this was not, in fact, borne out by the figures. The answer was not to rely on further very large contracts, but to develop France's day-to-day commercial links with South Africa over a wide range of products. French imports from South Africa in 1980 were value at F5,087m. Of this total, F4,508m fell into only six of the categories used by the French Customs (see Table 3 above).

Since French imports of South African coal have occasioned much comment, it is worth looking at this particular item in some detail. As South African coal is far cheaper than any obtainable elsewhere, it has been French policy to increase this trade, which has risen from only about one million tons in 1975. However, despite the cost advantage, over-reliance on one source would be quite out of tune with French policy.

The reliance on foreign coal dates from 1968, when the French decided it was uneconomic to go on producing 50–60 million tons annually and embarked on a very rapid programme of mine closures, designed to reduce domestic production to 15 million tons a year by 1980. In 1979 domestic

Table 4   France's principal suppliers of coal, coke and anthracite, 1980

	Amount in thousands of tonnes			Cost per tonne in F		
	Coal	Coke	Anthracite	Coal	Coke	Anthracite
South Africa	7,965*	672	599	195	287	302
West Germany	2,606	2,255	531	249	286	418
USSR	15	—	749	314	—	473
Britain	1,266	—	266	256	—	307
USA	3,357	3,953	245	230	286	391
Poland	2,735	819	7	228	284	361
Australia	436	1,044	106	207	285	208
Total above	18,380	8,743	2,503			
Total French imports	18,535	8,743	2,534			
Imports from SA as % of total	43.3 (40.8)†	7.7 (1.8)†	23.9 (27.4)†			

(1978 figures in brackets)

* This includes 85 per cent of France's imports (1,556,000 total) of lean coal.
† 1978 figures.

Source: Derived from *Statistiques du Commerce Extérieur de la France, 1980*.

production was reported to be 22 million tons, against imports of 25.4 million.[55] Pits affected are mostly in the Pas-de-Calais, but the reductions have caused relatively little labour trouble, though in September 1979 two hundred miners, supported by the French Communist Party, did occupy a ship laden with coal from South Africa, protesting, it appears, against foreign imports, rather than South African policies.[56]

The short-term consequences would be serious if South African coal were lost to France overnight, particularly as France suffers from an absolute lack of generating capacity. That position will change in the early 1980s, when a 'burn plateau' for coal will be reached, after which any increase will be supplied by nuclear energy. The dependence on South African coal may in part explain why France was the least prepared of the five Western powers negotiating with South Africa over Namibia to employ sanctions as an aid to negotiations (though alternative supplies of some other raw materials might be much less readily available). As it is, there is no large coal stockpile, partly because it would be difficult to store, and partly because no interruption in supply is foreseen. Table 4 compares South Africa with the more important of France's other suppliers of coal, coke and anthracite.

The other category of import deserving close attention is 26, which covers essential minerals. South Africa supplies 36 per cent by value of France's manganese (compare Gabon 44 per cent), 15 per cent of its lead (below Sweden and Morocco and just above Greenland), 32 per cent of its chrome (the other important suppliers being the Malagasy Republic (23 per cent), Turkey (18 per cent), Albania (12 per cent) and the USSR (6 per cent)) and 61 per cent of its titanium (with Australia the next supplier). South Africa also supplies small quantities of ilmenite, antimony and zirconium.

Uranium figures are not available for 1980. However, in 1978 natural uranium (F422m) and compounds of natural and of enriched uranium (F145m) accounted for 98.7 per cent of French imports from South Africa

Table 5   Major French exports to South Africa, 1980

Customs category	Shortenened title	Value in Fm
73	Steel and cast iron	354
84	Boilers & mechanical appliances	2,037
85	Electrical goods	437
87	Vehicles	345
	TOTAL	3,173

Source: Statistiques du Commerce Extérieur de a France, 1980.

in this category. South Africa supplied 51 per cent of France's natural uranium (the next source being Niger, with 14 per cent), but only 16 per cent of the compounds. Two kinds of uranium ore are imported. Type 1 has a uranium content of over 5 per cent and is imported exclusively from Gabon – 1,426 tonnes, value F439m. Type 2 is described as 'uranium ore: other', and 30 per cent of France's requirement is supplied by South Africa, almost all the remainder coming from Niger.

French exports to South Africa in 1980 totalled F4,071m, or 80 per cent of imports. Four principal categories accounted for F3,173m, or 78 per cent of total exports (see Table 5 above).

In 1975–8, both ships and aircraft were important export categories. In Table 6, South Africa's percentage of France's total exports in those categories is shown in the second column under each year.

Table 6   Ships and aircraft sold to South Africa, 1975–8, in Fm, and as percentage of total French exports in those categories

	1975		1976		1977		1978	
	Fm	%	Fm	%	Fm	%	Fm	%
Ships	2.6	0.1	33.0	1.4	365	15.0	815	26.6
Aircraft	166.9	9.2	648.1	27.5	465	19.1	36.6*	1.0

* Almost entirely spare parts.
Source: CFCE, *Afrique du Sud* (Paris, 1979), pp. 72 and 73, and *Statistiques du Commerce Extérieur de la France, 1978.*

It should be noted that the French and, e.g., the British arms industries operate differently, in that the former produces with exports in mind from the beginning, and then persuades the French armed forces to adopt them, whereas British arms are made primarily for British needs. (French arms sales are not necessarily very profitable. Those to, for example, the Francophone African states are heavily subsidized.)

As far as bank loans are concerned, the French anti-apartheid movement, despite the unwillingness of such bodies as Iscor (Iron and Steel Corporation) to publicize loans, has identified 176 Western loans to the South African government and parastatals in the period 1950–78, of which French banks participated in 57, all but three to parastatals.[57] The movement has included only those loans of which it is certain; it is reasonably sure that there have been many others, but the evidence is inadequate. Destinations were:

Parastatals*	112
Government	26
Mines	13
Local authorities	7
Bantustans	3
Various	15
	176

*Escom 42, Iscor 29, SArh 20, Idc 9, Post Office 3, SABC 3, Safmarine 2, Strategic Oil Fund 1, Foskor 1, Richards Bay 1 (1 not listed).

I return now to the discussion of some policy issues: the EC's Code of Conduct, the arms embargo and the stockpiling of minerals.

The Code of Conduct

The code has been discussed regularly by the EC states in Political Co-operation, and clear differences of view have emerged between Britain and France. The British believe that, since the code is one of the few constructive joint measures to have been agreed by the Nine in relation to South Africa, the most should be made of it. In particular, publicity should be given to companies' reports, and some sort of joint assessment should be made by the Ten (effectively, however, only Britain, France and Germany) of the code's operation and effectiveness, though this would not necessarily be made public.

The French are firmly opposed to the latter proposal, since, although they insist that the practice of French firms has long equalled, or indeed surpassed, the standards enjoined by the code, they believe the code to be little short of a waste of time. It may well be suitable for British businessmen, who are accustomed to filling in forms, but it is of little relevance to France, which in any case only has about twenty-five affected companies (a reflection no doubt of the French emphasis on local manufacture under licence, and other forms of association with South African-based firms), and some of these have few, if any, black employees. Furthermore, since there is no obligation upon companies to report and the code itself is voluntary, it is very difficult to persuade companies to take any interest in it, particularly in the absence of any significant interested public opinion (e.g., French students are no more concerned with South Africa than are English ones with Algeria). If, however, enough companies do report (which seems unlikely, since no effort is being made to encourage them to do so), the individual reports will remain unpublished. They will be submitted in the first instance to the CFCE, which will pass them on to the Direction des Relations Economiques Extérieures (DREE), which is a subdivision of the Ministry of the Economy and of the Ministry of Foreign Trade, and the DREE will, in turn, publish a report based upon all of them. Even if that point were reached, however, it appears that the French would be unwilling to cooperate in any international assessment.

The arms embargo

Whatever its record in the past, it does seem that France now observes the existing arms embargo, though doubts have been expressed about spare parts, and Moroccan arms are said to have reached South Africa. (France's earlier sales of arms are recorded in the *Notes and Documents* series of the UN Centre against Apartheid.)

There are three procedures by which arms sales are controlled. First, they are overseen by an interministerial committee, where deadlocks are resolved by the prime minister. A company has to obtain permission from this committee (*a*) to start negotiations; (*b*) to conclude a deal; (*c*) physically to export the arms. The list of arms to which these requirements apply is revised periodically.

The second procedure is less strict. A list was issued in about 1977 contained in an 'avis aux exportateurs des matériaux sensibles' under which the Ministry of Industry is to be informed of all dealings in 'matériaux sensibles' – that is, in goods which could have military application. This is advice rather than instruction, but it is generally followed, in view of the extent of administrative control which government can exercise over the commercial system.

Third, a group headed by the Secretary-General of the Quai d'Orsay (Groupe Interministérielle pour les Matériaux Sensibles) considers all nuclear exports. Its decisions are, again, strictly binding only on sellers owned by the government.

Mineral stockpiles

France has long experience of stockpiling, since the oil law of 1928 provides for it. The 1974 budget provided for stockpiling raw materials and purchasing started the following year. By 1979 only F300m had been spent[58] – most of it, if not all, it is believed, on copper – but in that year the French government decided greatly to increase the stockpile. Purchases are made through the Groupement des Achats des Métaux Non-Ferreux, which in theory (though not in fact) was abandoned under the Treaty of Rome. A further decision was taken in 1979 to go on stockpiling, but this time it was not to be financed from the budget, in view of the then current 'squeeze'. Instead, a government loan stock in the form of ten-year bonds was issued to finance acquisitions.[59]

The French are undoubtedly taking the minerals question seriously, and an interministerial working party has studied supplies of minerals from the whole of Africa. The available supply figures are rather meagre, but it is clear that France's position is far more favourable than is that of Germany. The former (if one includes New Caledonia) was self-sufficient in aluminium, iron ore, nickel and cobalt (though the last not in 1978, owing to greatly increased consumption), and about 50 per cent self-sufficient in lead and platinum (the latter from recycling). German and French figures are not strictly comparable, since the French realistically include the products of recycling when calculating their degree of dependence. Thus, although France produces no platinum, it claims about 50 per cent autonomy because 82 per cent of its consumption comes from recycling, whereas the Germans would regard platinum as an example of total dependence on imports.[60] A prime concern is to continue the policy of diversification, with, for example, copper and lead from Brittany, nickel from New Caledonia, chrome from Turkey, cobalt from Morocco.

It is emphasized that the stockpiles now contemplated are to protect French industry against shortages, *not* with a view to a war in which France might be involved. Nevertheless, the details are handled with the utmost secrecy. No figures of stocks or intended stocks are released, and even the crumb of information that the stocks are intended to cover two months' needs (over and above the stocks normally held by industry) is valueless, since this is only an average period and different targets are set for different minerals on the list. (It is known that the uranium stock is very large.) Nor is the list itself published, though it is known to be much more extensive than the German. It may be assumed to include cobalt and the four South African minerals on the German list, plus, according to *The Economist*, at least antimony, titanium and zirconium, the last because of its importance in building nuclear reactors.[61] Nor are the targets immutable – they may be raised or lowered in the light of events. It is stressed that, if stocks are released to French industry, the purpose will not be to give French entrepreneurs an advantage over foreign competitors, but to provide stocks on the same terms as competitors enjoy. That is, if a competitor benefits from a long-term, fixed-price contract, the French authorities would match those conditions but not improve on them. Officials state that storage presents no problem. Stocks are stored partly by industry, but mostly by government.

The secrecy surrounding the stockpile may partly be explained by the need not to distort the markets: indeed, one may speculate that the emphasis laid, both in France and in Germany (until the latter shelved its plans), on the very lengthy legal and financial cogitation that must precede major operations may be a 'cover' for operations already taking place. On the other hand, since the South African government prides itself on being able to chart the progress of stockpiles, the concern may indeed be, as is claimed, to protect commercial rather than national security.

Conclusion

Under President Giscard d'Estaing there did not appear to be a settled government view of the desirability, or otherwise, of increased investment in and trade with South Africa. On the whole, though, it seems probable that, despite the President's personal distaste for the South African system, some ministers shared the view expressed in business circles that trade and investment should be increased, provided it was done quietly. Nor is there evidence that the Nigerian 'threat' was taken seriously, although Nigeria is France's largest trading partner in Africa (if one excludes the Maghreb), followed by Ivory Coast and South Africa. (It is, however, worth noting that Nigeria's reputation for paying for its imports is not uniformly good in France or in Britain. Trade statistics refer to physical movements of goods, not to payments.)

On the other hand, there was an awareness that vote-counting in the United Nations is important, particularly in relation to France's continuing presence in New Caledonia and Réunion. Furthermore, it was argued by some that alternative markets could easily be found and the loss of trade with South Africa would have no perceptible adverse consequences for employment in France. It follows from this view (which is, of course, opposed to that of the many business and government leaders who, as noted earlier, think there are good reasons for increased trade) that, because there is no political or emotional 'constituency', increased trade with South Africa is in a sense irrational; there is even some doubt whether Giscard's government would have extended official insurance to Koeberg in the political climate of 1979 or 1980. In short, as one might expect, the political and official worlds were no less disunited than in Britain on these questions. It can, however, be said with confidence that all things being equal, French bureaucrats and politicians were fully alive to the need to maintain freedom of movement and so were likely to express support for moves made by Britain and the USA, or by other states of the EC acting within the framework of Political Cooperation.

The last remains true under President Mitterrand. There is clearly, as we have seen, a difference in emphasis between the Socialist Party's and the government's formulation of South African policy. Nevertheless, the government, though naturally sensitive to party views, will continue to play its part, perhaps a more lively part, in the Contact Group; it will, no doubt, seek to play down and render less cordial its relations with South Africa, but it is likely to continue to leave major initiatives to others.

References

Chapter 2: The International Setting

1 Hugh Tinker, *Race, Conflict and the International Order* (London, Macmillan, 1977), p. 132.
2 Quoted in James Barber, 'Sanctions Against Rhodesia', Open University Course D233, *World Politics*, Block III, Paper 6 (Open University Press, 1981), p. 19.
3 South African House of Assembly debates, 23 March 1961, cols. 3501-2.
4 Speech at UN Human Rights seminar, 23 June 1970, Zambia Information Services, Background Paper No. 47/70.
5 Keesing's Contemporary Archives, 12 Aug. 1977, col. 28507.
6 Richard Bissell, *Apartheid and International Organizations* (Boulder, Colo., Westview Press, 1977), p. 171.
7 Ronald Segal, ed., *Sanctions Against South Africa* (Harmondsworth, Penguin, 1964), p. 14.
8 Foreign and Commonwealth Office, *Report of the Supply of Petroleum and Petroleum Products to Rhodesia* [Bingham Report] (HMSO, 1978), p. 105.
9 David Scott, *Ambassador in Black and White* (London, Weidenfeld & Nicolson, 1981), p. 195.
10 *The Guardian*, 12 Oct. 1977.
11 Barry Cohen and Mohamed A. El-Khawas, eds., *The Kissinger Study on Southern Africa* (Nottingham, Spokesman Books, 1975), p. 46.
12 Henry Kissinger, 'The Special Relationship', *The Listener*, 13 May 1982, p. 16.
13 *The Times*, 31 Aug. 1981.

Chapter 3: The Economic Stake

1 Ruth First, Jonathan Steele and Christabel Gurney, *The South African Connection* (Harmondsworth, Penguin, 1973), p. 23.
2 John McQuiggan, 'The Comparative Importance to British Businessmen of Trade with South Africa and Trade with the Rest of Africa', talk to the South Africa Institute of International Affairs, 11 Feb. 1981 (mimeograph).
3 Rodney Stares and Martin Bailey, *British Banks and South Africa* (London, Christian Concern for Southern Africa, 1978; hereafter CCSA), p. 30.
4 Personal conversations.
5 R. W. Johnson, *How Long Will South Africa Survive?* (London, Macmillan, 1977), p. 28.
6 First, *et al.*, op. cit., pp. 14–15.
7 *Rand Daily Mail*, 9 Oct. 1980.

8 Consolidated Gold Fields, *Annual Report 1980*, p. 12.
9 Johnson, op. cit., p. 216.
10 *Rand Daily Mail*, 9 Oct. 1980.
11 *South African Financial Times*, 24 Sept. 1980.
12 Bernard Rivers and Martin Bailey, *Britain's Economic Links with South Africa* (London, CCSA, 1979).
13 Stares and Bailey, op. cit., outlines the development of South African banks.
14 Sir Julian Crossley and John Blandford, *The DCO Story* (London, Barclays Bank International, 1975), p. 283.
15 Stares and Bailey, op. cit., p.31.
16 Greg Lanning, with Marti Mueller, *Africa Undermined* (Harmondsworth, Penguin, 1979), p. 277.
17 Estimate by Phillip Crowson. See his *Non-fuel Minerals and Foreign Policy* (London, Royal Institute of International Affairs, 1977).
18 Rivers and Bailey, op. cit., p. 32.
19 See Lanning, op. cit., p. 109.
20 Quoted in Barber, 'Sanctions Against Rhodesia' (see ch. 2, n. 2, above), p. 42.
21 Rivers and Bailey, op. cit., and UKSATA, *British Trade with South Africa: A Question of National Interest* (UKSATA, 1978).
22 UKSATA, op. cit., para. 8(3).

Chapter 4: The Search for Values

1 See Hedley Bull, *The Anarchical Society* (London, Macmillan, 1977), ch. 4, and James Barber, 'Justice and Order in International Politics: The Case of South Africa', *Millennium*, vol. 8, no. 2, Autumn 1979.
2 See Bull, op. cit., p. 85. As examples Bull gives the prevention of nuclear war and the preservation of the environment.
3 Sir Alec Douglas-Home, Address to Conservative Party Conference, 9 Oct. 1970 (verbatim report, Chatham House Press Library).
4 Published by Oxford University Press, under the same title, in 1979.
5 24 Jan. 1979, verbatim service 7/79, Chatham House Press Library.
6 *Human Rights* (London, Jonathan Cape, 1978), p. 92.
7 British Council of Churches, *Violence in Southern Africa: A Christian Assessment* (BCC, 1970).
8 Published by Heinemann, under the same title, in 1980.
9 Ibid., p. 36.
10 Bailey later published a full-scale study of the breaking of oil sanctions, *Oilgate* (Coronet Books, 1979).
11 See *The Guardian*, 12 March 1973, for the first of these.
12 *The Times*, 22 March 1973.
13 House of Commons, Fifth Report from the Expenditure Committee, Trade and Industry Sub-Committee, 1973–4 Session, 'Wages and Conditions of African Workers Employed by British Firms in South Africa' (HMSO, 1974).
14 David Butler and Michael Pinto-Duschinsky, *The British General Election of 1970* (London, Macmillan, 1971).
15 Harold Wilson, *The Labour Government 1964–70* (Harmondsworth, Penguin, 1974), p. 985.
16 David Butler and Dennis Kavanagh, *The British General Election of February 1974* (London, Macmillan, 1974); *The British General Election of October 1974*

(London, Macmillan, 1975); and *The British General Election of 1979* (London, Macmillan, 1980).

17 Richard Crossman, *The Diaries of a Cabinet Minister,* vol. 1 (London, Hamish Hamilton and Jonathan Cape, 1975), p. 432.

18 Kenneth Waltz, *Foreign Policy and Domestic Policy* (London, Longman, 1968), p. 45.

19 *The Guardian,* 26 Oct. 1977.

20 *The Times,* 1 Sept. 1981.

21 M. Laing, *Edward Heath* (London, Sidgwick & Jackson, 1972), p. 181.

22 Philip Norton, *Conservative Dissidents: Dissent within the Parliamentary Conservative Party 1970-74* (London, Temple Smith, 1978), pp. 125-6.

23 Ibid., pp. 41-2.

24 *The Times,* 12 Oct. 1978.

25 George Brown, *In My Way* (London, Gollancz, 1971), p. 174.

26 Crossman, op. cit., vol. 3, p. 671.

27 *Hansard,* vol. 801, col. 1060, 12 May 1970.

28 Ibid., vol. 804, col. 600, 22 July 1970.

29 *The Times,* 30 Sept. 1970.

30 *The Times,* 29 Nov. 1974.

31 *The Financial Times,* 4 Oct. 1979.

32 *The Times,* 5 Oct. 1978.

33 Ibid., 30 Sept. 1977.

Chapter 5: Pressure Groups

1 A brief account of the development of the AAM is in George Shepherd, *Anti-Apartheid* (London, Greenwood Press, 1977), p. 25.

2 AAM Constitution, sect. 2.

3 AAM, *Annual Report 1978-9,* p. 22.

4 AAM, *Annual Report 1979-80,* p. 23.

5 Ibid, p. 15.

6 AAM, *Annual Report 1978-9,* p. 9.

7 AAM, *Annual Report 1977-8,* p. 19.

8 Ibid., p. 24.

9 AAM, *Annual Report 1979-80,* p. 20.

10 Richard Gibson, *African Liberation Movements* (London, Oxford University Press, 1972), p. 69.

11 *Britain's Economic Stake in Apartheid* (AAM, June 1979).

12 AAM, *Annual Report 1972-3,* p. 2.

13 *The Anti-Apartheid Movement's Perspective for the 1980s* (AAM, June 1979).

14 AAM, *Annual Report 1978-9,* p. 13.

15 See, for instance, Bailey, *Oilgate.*

16 *South African Financial Mail,* 7 Dec. 1973.

17 *The Collaborators* (AAM, 1963, with a Foreword by Barbara Castle), p. 17.

18 South Africa Foundation (SAF), *Annual Report 1978-9,* p. 13.

19 SAF, Presidential Address by Major-General Sir Francis de Guingand (South Africa Foundation, 1971), p. 1.

20 SAF, *Annual Report 1980-1,* pp. 2-9.

21 De Guingand, op. cit., pp. 2-3.

22 *South Africa Foundation News,* vol. 4, no. 3, March 1978.

23 SAF, *Annual Report 1980-1*, p. 2.

24 *Rand Daily Mail*, 25 March 1980.

25 *The Financial Times*, 14 March 1980.

26 SAF, *Annual Report 1978-9*, p. 22.

27 *Hansard* (Lords), 26 April 1978, vol. 390, col. 1913.

28 *Hansard*, 25 May 1979, vol. 967, col. 1387-8.

29 These are contained in the UKSATA pamphlet: *British Trade with South Africa*, paras. 15-20.

30 Quoted by First, *et al.*, op. cit., p. 219.

31 *The Times*, 16 Jan. 1970.

32 First, *et al.*, op. cit., p. 218.

33 Ibid., p. 219.

34 Paras. 21 and 26.

35 Full text of speech by Mr Peter Blaker at the Café Royal, 4 Dec. 1979, circulated by UKSATA.

36 *The Future of South Africa* (BCC International Division, 1965).

37 *Violence in Southern Africa - A Christian Assessment* (BCC International Division, 1970).

38 *The Programme to Combat Racism* (World Council of Churches, n.d.).

39 *Investment in Southern Africa* (BCC International Division, 1973).

40 *Political Change in Southern Africa: Britain's Responsibility* (BCC International Division, 1979).

41 CCSA, *Annual Reports* (London, 1977 and 1978).

42 These detailed proposals were set out in an appendix to the main resolution of the BCC Assembly, 21 Nov. 1979.

43 An account of the banning of D and AF is given in *The Daily Telegraph* 19 March 1966, which prompted a vigorous correspondence.

44 *The Sunday Times*, 4 Oct. 1981.

45 See Gordon Winter, *Inside BOSS* (Harmondsworth, Penguin, 1981).

46 Martin Bailey, 'BOSS at work in Britain', *New Statesman*, 15 Aug. 1980.

47 Hansard, 9 March 1976, vol. 907, col. 246-7. See also Barrie Penrose and Roger Courtiour, *The Pencourt File* (London, Secker and Warburg, 1978).

Chapter 6: Decision-makers and Policy Options

1 D. G. Clarke, *Economic Sanctions on South Africa: Past Evidence and Future Potential* (Geneva, International University Exchange Fund, 1980), pp. 8-14.

2 *The Times*, 26 Aug. 1981.

3 Peter Hain, *Don't Play with Apartheid* (London, George Allen & Unwin, 1971), p. 104.

4 Quoted in *Rand Daily Mail*, 11 Oct. 1980.

5 William Wallace, *The Foreign Policy Process in Britain* (London, George Allen & Unwin, for the Royal Institute of International Affairs, 1976) pp. 6 and 9.

6 *Hansard*, 8 Dec. 1978, vol. 959, col. 1738.

7 Ibid., col. 1825.

8 *Hansard*, 4 Dec. 1974, vol. 882, col. 1555.

9 *Hansard*, 10 Nov. 1977, vol. 938, col. 830.

10 *The Daily Telegraph*, 19 Dec. 1979.

11 Richard Luce, Under-Secretary of State for Foreign and Commonwealth

Affairs, told the Commons: 'We believe in a policy of contact and dialogue between our two Governments as the most constructive approach.' *Hansard,* 29 Oct. 1980, vol. 991, col. 471.

12 Crossman, *The Diaries of a Cabinet Minister,* vol. 1, p. 377.

13 Scott, *Ambassador in Black and White,* p. 181.

14 House of Commons, Fifth Report from the Expenditure Committee, 1973–4 Session 'Wages and Conditions of African Workers Employed by British Firms in South Africa' (HMSO, 1974).

15 Ibid. The Department of Trade and Industry's memo is reprinted in the *Minutes of Evidence,* vol. 1, pp. 338–40. The questioning of the officials is in the same volume, pp. 340–50. The sub-committee's report is published in a separate volume, in which Chapter 12 is 'The Basis for our Recommendations', and Chapter 13 is 'Recommendations'.

16 Foreign and Commonwealth Office, *Report of the Supply of Petroleum and Petroleum Products to Rhodesia* [The Bingham Report] (HMSO, 1978).

17 Quoted in Barber, 'Sanctions Against Rhodesia' (see ch. 2, n. 2, above), p. 42.

18 Bingham Report, Annex 2, p. 240.

19 Geoffrey Berridge, *Economic Power in Anglo-South African Diplomacy* (London, Macmillan, 1981), pp. 64–5.

20 Ibid., p. 165.

21 George Brown, *In My Way* (London, Gollancz, 1971), pp. 170–4.

22 Crossman, op. cit., vol. 2, p. 476.

23 Harold Wilson, *The Labour Government 1964–70: A Personal Record* (London, Weidenfeld/Michael Joseph, 1971), p. 470.

24 Bingham Report, p. 107.

25 See H. Oppenheimer, 'Why the world should continue to invest in South Africa', supplement to *Optima,* no. 1, 1978. For a discussion of this and other options, see James Barber and Michael Spicer, 'Sanctions against South Africa – Options for the West', *International Affairs,* July 1979.

26 *The Times,* 31 Aug. 1981.

27 Henry Brandon, 'Botha responds to "carrot not stick" approach on Namibia', *Sunday Times,* 13 Sept. 1981.

28 David Owen, Speech to mark International Anti-Apartheid Year, 24 Jan. 1979, at Central Hall, Westminster. Verbatim report in Chatham House Press Library.

29 Simon Clarke, *Financial Aspects of Economic Sanctions on South Africa* (Geneva, International University Exchange Fund, 1980), p. 47.

30 Abdul S. Minty, *The Case for Economic Disengagement* (UN Centre Against Apartheid, 1976), no. 35, p. 76.

31 D. G. Clarke, *Policy Issues and Economic Sanctions on South Africa* (Geneva, International University Exchange Fund, 1980), p. 5.

32 James Barber, Jesmond Blumenfeld and Christopher R. Hill, *The West and South Africa* (London, Routledge & Kegan Paul, for the Royal Institute of International Affairs, 1982), Chatham House Paper No. 14, pp. 68–9.

33 For a discussion of 'core interest', see K. J. Holsti, *International Politics: A Framework for Analysis* (New Jersey, Prentice Hall, 3rd edn, 1977), pp. 145–8.

Appendix

1 Reinhardt Rummel, 'The Shift from Dogmatism to Pragmatism in the EC', *Aussenpolitik* (English edition), vol. 30 (1979), pp. 27, 28 and 29.

2 The point is developed by Manfred Heinrich and Klaus von der Ropp in 'Lomé II in the Light of Experience with Lomé I', *Aussenpolitik*, vol. 29 (1978), pp. 301–2.

3 Some of these speeches are reprinted in H. D. Genscher, *Deutsche Aussenpolitik* (Stuttgart, Verlag Bonn Aktuell, 1977).

4 See Zdenak Cervenka and Mario R. Dederichs, 'The Two Germanies in Africa: Eastern Advances and Western Isolation', in *Africa Contemporary Record*, 1979, p. A147.

5 Institut für Internationale Begegnungen, *Newsletter* (Bonn), 21 Aug. 1980.

6 Ibid., 3 Nov. 1980.

7 Ibid., 15 Dec. 1980.

8 Ibid., 1 April 1981. The meeting was between SWAPO and the Interessengemeinschaft der Deutschen Südwester (IG) and was interpreted in some South African press comment as a move against the Democratic Turnhalle Alliance (DTA); see, e.g., *Die Transvaler*, 12 Jan. 1981.

9 For the affair of the military attaché, see *Frankfurter Allegemeine Zeitung*, 2 and 3 Nov. 1979, and *Rand Daily Mail*, 10 Nov. 1979.

10 T. Hanf, H. Weiland and G. Vierdag, *South Africa: The Prospects of Peaceful Change* (London, Rex Collings; Cape Town, David Philip; and Bloomington, Indiana University Press, 1981).

11 For a useful discussion of French policy and the strains it might produce in the Western alliance, see Winrich Kühne, 'Die Französische Afrika Politik' in *Aus Politik und Zeitgeschichte* (Bonn, Bundeszentrale für Politische Bildung, 1979).

12 *Africa Cofidential*, vol. 22, no. 14, 1 July 1981.

13 See, e.g., *Beeld*, 12 May 1981, and *Die Transvaler*, 13 May 1981.

14 *Africa Confidential*, vol. 22, no. 12, 13 June 1981, and vol. 22, no. 14, 1 July 1981.

15 Ibid., 1 Sept. 1981.

16 French Embassy, London, *Note d'Actualité*, 24 July 1980, reprinting speech by M. François-Poncet in Tanzania, 19 July 1980 (M. François-Poncet took this opportunity to emphasize France's wish 'to expand her relations with the countries of east and southern Africa, with which she has no traditional ties'), and 12 Sept. 1980.

17 *Note d'Actualité*, 28 July 1980.

18 Ibid., 29 May 1981.

19 Ibid., 4 June 1981.

20 Ibid., 22 June 1981. Compare 1967–8, when de Gaulle's sharp reversal of policy towards Israel and the Arab world suffered from no such inhibitions.

21 For a useful set of documents, see Südafrikanische Kirchenrat und Evangelische Kirche in Deutschland, *Wirtschaftsbeziehungen zu Südafrika* (1978).

22 For a note of the scheme, see C. R. Hill, 'Aid for South Africa', *The Tablet*, 2 June 1979, pp. 527–8.

23 Federal Press and Information Office, *Fact v. Fiction: Rebuttal of the Charges of Alleged Cooperation between the Federal Republic of Germany and South*

Africa in the Nuclear and Military Fields (Bonn, 1978).

24 *Bericht des Staatssekretärausschusses für Rohstofffragen über Risiken der Rohstoffversorgung und Möglichkeiten einer staatlichen Krisenversorge an das Kabinett,* unpublished paper presented to the Federal German cabinet in November 1978.

25 Bundesminister für Wirtschaft (BMWI), *Metals and Minerals – Markets and Trends* (Bonn, 1979), pp. 34, 35 and 39.

26 South African–German Chamber of Trade and Industry (Chamber), *Annual Report 1980* (Johannesburg), p. 54.

27 Ibid., p. 55.

28 State Secretaries report, op. cit. (n. 24 above), and BMWI, op. cit., pp. 101–6.

29 For the text of the report, see A. Akeroyd, F. Ansprenger, R. Hermle and C. R. Hill (eds.), *European Business and South Africa: An Appraisal of the EC Code of Conduct* (Mainz, Matthias-Grünewald-Verlag, 1981), pp. 150–9.

30 During a joint meeting of the Bundestag's Economic and Foreign Affairs Committee on 23 June 1980, the government was repeatedly urged by SPD members and academic witnesses both to use stronger persuasion to ensure compliance with the code and to publish individual companies' reports. Business attitudes were also fully expressed during the hearing.

31 For an account of the report, see *Frankfurter Allgemeine Zeitung* and *Rand Daily Mail,* 10 Oct. 1979.

32 Total German direct investment abroad from 1952 to end 1979 was DM66,000m. See Chamber, *Annual Report 1980,* p. 80. South Africa was Germany's seventeenth most important field for investment, and Germany ranked third below Britain and the USA in the list of foreign investors (ibid., p. 41).

33 Deutsche Bundesbank, 'Stand der Directinvestitionen 1976' in *Monatsberichte der Deutschen Bundesbank* (Bonn, Federal German Press and Information Office, April 1979), pp. 26–40.

34 Chamber, *Annual Report 1977/8,* p. 38.

35 Chamber, *Annual Report 1980,* p. 44.

36 Chamber, *Annual Report 1977/8,* p. 10.

37 *Rand Daily Mail,* 19 Oct. 1979.

38 Ibid., 28 Jan. 1980.

39 Chamber, *Annual Report 1980,* p. 43.

40 Ibid.

41 I am indebted to Mr Jesmond Blumenfeld for these figures. See J. P. Barber, J. Blumenfeld and C. R. Hill, *The West and South Africa* (Routledge and Kegan Paul, for the Royal Insitute of International Affairs, 1982).

42 German official trade statistics.

43 See Cervenka and Dederichs, op. cit. (n. 4 above).

44 See, however, the Afrikaans press of 25 Aug. 1981 for widespread adverse reaction to an apparent attempt by the French ambassador to lead a Western démarche, condemning the South African government for its treatment of squatters in the Cape Peninsula.

45 See, however, Galen Hull, 'The French Connection in Africa: Zaire and South Africa', *Journal of Southern African Studies,* vol. 5 (April 1979, pp. 220–33. Hull concludes (p. 232) that 'French interests in South Africa are

increasingly defined in terms of the need for access to vital raw materials'.

46 R. Lefort, 'Révisions Françaises en Afrique Australe', in *Regards sur l'Actualité* (Paris, Documentation Française, December 1977), p. 12.

47 See, for example, Christian Concern for Southern Africa, *Britain's Economic Links with South Africa* (London, 1979).

48 Centre Français du Commerce Extérieur (CFCE), *Afrique du Sud*, Dossier d'Information de Base (Paris, 1979) pp. 169–70.

49 Centre de Recherches et d'Information sur l'Afrique Australe (CRIAA), *Votre banque et l'apartheid* (Paris, 1978).

50 Lefort, op. cit., p. 7.

51 *Africa Confidential*, vol. 22, no. 14, 1 July 1981.

52 *The Financial Times*, 10 July 1979.

53 CRIAA, op. cit., p. 10.

54 CFCE, op. cit., p. 167.

55 *L'Humanité*, 20 Sept. 1979.

56 *The Daily Telegraph*, 20 Sept. 1979. For a suggestion that anti-apartheid protests were also involved, see *Rand Daily Mail*, 22 Sept. 1979.

57 CRIAA, op. cit., pp. 36 and 38.

58 *The Economist*, 2 June 1979, p. 85.

59 *Africa Confidential*, vol. 22, no. 13, 17 June 1981.

60 Ministère de l'Industrie, *Les Chiffres clés des matières premières minérales, 1979* (Paris, 1979).

61 *The Economist*, loc. cit.

Index